Wildlife Sketches

By

G.W. Bradt
Charles E. Schafer
Steve Harrington

Wildlife Sketches
Published previously by the Michigan Department of Natural Resources as *Michigan Wildlife Sketches.*
By: G.W. Bradt, Charles E. Schafer, and Steve Harrington

ISBN: 0-9625629-3-4

Contents

Introduction

Wildlife Sketches was first published by the Michigan Department of Natural Resources in 1947. Through the years it has retained its place as an authoritative source of general information about mammals of the Great Lakes region.

With this edition, the book has been drastically updated and expanded to provide more up-to-date information about wildlife. It is interesting to note that in many cases, species have actually expanded their ranges so they are more common now than when the book was first published.

New information about wildlife ecology has been added to give readers a better understanding about how wild animals relate to their environments and human pressures.

Wildlife Sketches continues to offer solid information about wild animals throughout the Great Lakes region. Perhaps some day these pages will tell even more stories about how man has helped wild animals prosper in the region.

The Opossum--
Invader From the South...

The opossum is a comparative newcomer to Michigan, having been absent or very rare in pioneer times. There are some records of the opossum in Michigan in the early 1800's, but they seem to have disappeared completely about 1860, and reappeared about the time of World War I. Since about 1927, they have become widely distributed in the southern portions of the Great Lakes region.

Although the 'possum is considered an important game animal in the southern states, particularly in that part of the south called Dixie, it never gained much popularity in this region. This is probably due partly to its appearance of ungainly stupidity, and partly to its unsavory reputation as a robber of chicken roosts and nests. The shambling gait, rat-like tail, snarling, toothy "grin," beady eyes and unkempt coat, all detract from its "personality," and create an unfavorable comparison with its woodland neighbor, the handsome, intelligent and "cute" raccoon.

A Sort of Living Fossil

Perhaps no modern description of Br'er 'Possum has been better than that of Captain John Smith who reported that: "the opossum hath a head like a swine, a tayle like a rate, as bigge as a cat, and bath under her belly a bag wherein she carrieth her young."

Actually, we should look on the poor, stupid, old 'possum with considerable respect, for he is a sort of living fossil, a veritable Methuselah among mammals, and most of his relatives have been true fossils these past million years or more. Moreover, the 'possum today is not just a highly modified modern descendant of the fossil 'possums of a million years ago, he still looks just about like his remote ancestors.

So little change has taken place through the ages that an opossum skull from the ancient rock formations of Wyoming can scarcely be distinguished from that of an opossum from a hollow tree today. Why has the opossum remained like his fossil ancestors for millenniums, while other mammals have become highly modified and "modernized" to meet changing conditions of climate and geography? Slow, stupid, weak, with no special equipment for competition, why does he still exist and even extend his range? The answer is really rather simple, he eats anything and everything, animal or vegetable, dead or alive; and produces lots and lots of offspring.

Young Are Carried in Pouch

Opossums are marsupial mammals. That is, the females possess a pouch in which the young are carried and nursed during infancy. This characteristic is shared only with the kangaroos and other mammals of far away Australia and nearby islands. Every native mammal of Australia is a marsupial, but the only other marsupials on earth are the opossums of the Americas.

The gestation period of the opossum is less than two weeks, and the young, from five to 15 per litter ordinarily, are born in an extremely underdeveloped, almost embryonic condition. When first born, they are naked and flesh-colored, with eyes and ears covered with an integument, and the mouth a tiny opening almost pin point in size.

The average length of a new-born opossum is considerably less than an inch, tail and all, with a weight of less than a gram. These tiny creatures crawl, or are placed by the mother, inside the pouch, where they attach themselves to a nipple and grow fast there, remaining attached for about a month, when they reach a size and condition approximating that of other young mammals at birth.

Then they lose their attachment, crawl out of the pouch, and all over the mother. It is a comical sight to see a mother opossum walking or climbing with a dozen little ones hanging on her back and sides. Opossums are very good "hangers on," since their tails are prehensile, and can be used in swinging from a branch, or in carrying objects such as leaves or sticks.

The whole family of young remains with the mother about two months. In the meantime, a second brood may be produced, so that two or even more broods of different sizes may be seen accompanying the mother on her travels.

He Has Little Intelligence

One of the peculiar characteristics of the opossum, which has given rise to endless speculation, is his habit of "playing 'possum." Frequently, when an opossum is attached, or thinks he is about to be attacked, he will suddenly fall limp and inert, and draw back the gums from his long rows of glittering white teeth until he looks as if he might have been dead a month. One can roll him about with the foot, pick him up and carry him away by the tail, or offer him any indignity and he will not make a move. Were it not for his warmth and pulse one might really believe he was dead. But put him down and walk quietly away a few steps, then watch him closely. His little shoe-button eyes will open, and if he doesn't seen anything dangerous looking he will get up and go calmly about his business.

As to intelligence, most observers agree that the opossum has little. Ernest Thompson Seton tried an experiment to determine the relative brain capacity of various mammals. He used beans to fill the brain case of mammal skulls with the following results. It took 21 beans to fill an opossum brain case, 35 for a skunk, 46 for a hare, 70 for a porcupine, 150 for a raccoon, 198 for a fox, 325 for a coyote, and 438 for a wolf.

As to intelligence, most observers agree that the opossum has little.

Of course, the larger size of the fox, coyote, and wolf introduced another factor in the problem. However, the skunk, hare, and porcupine are not mental giants, and are about the size of an opossum, yet their brains are much larger. The raccoon, not much larger, but recognized as a smart trickster, had over seven times the brain capacity of the opossum. Seton concludes that this brain test corroborates

OPOSSUM

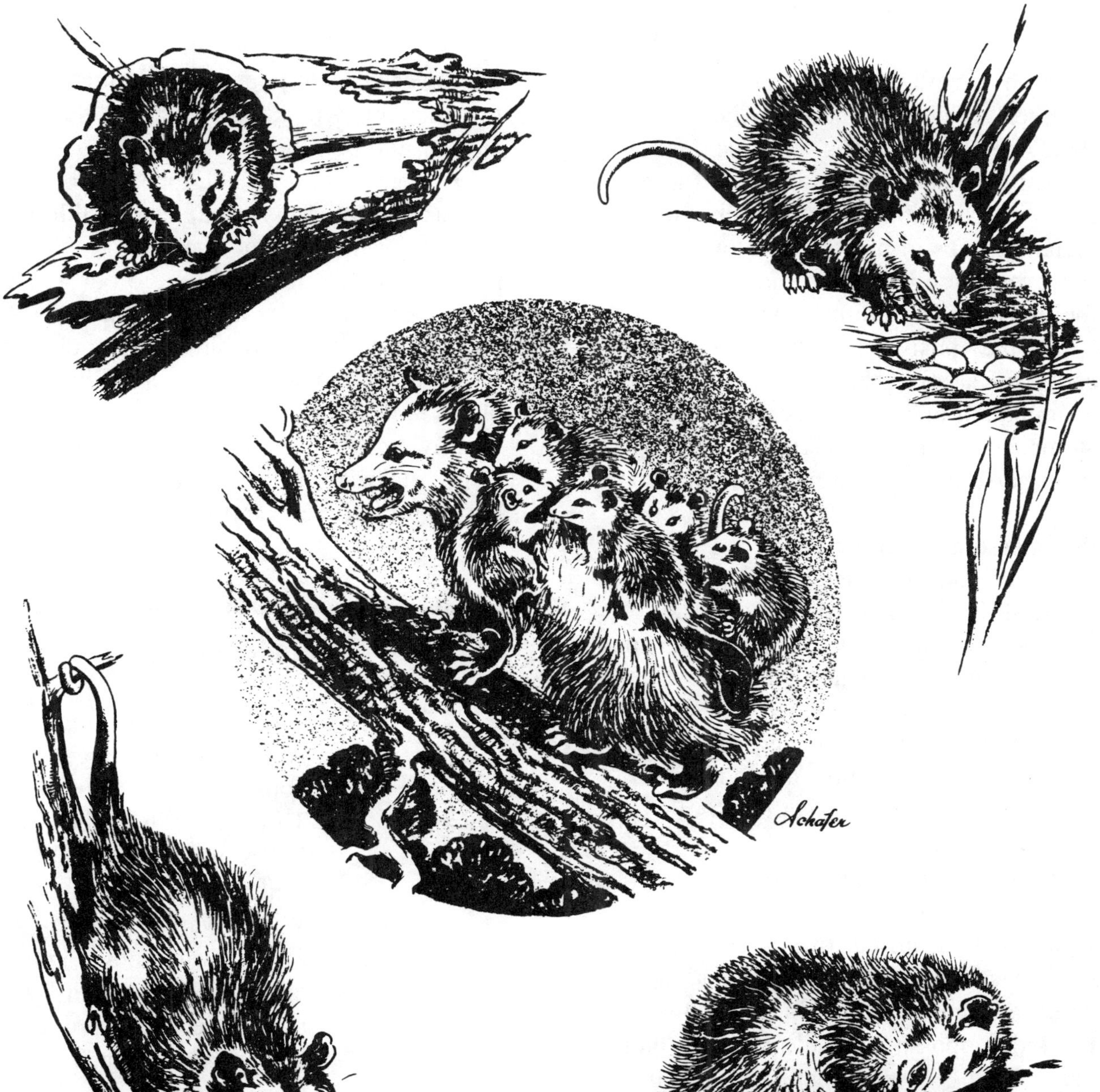

observations in the woods and characterizes the opossum as a "silly idiot."

Was Once a "Public Enemy"

From time to time, the opossum receives unfavorable publicity because of its alleged depredations on game animals. For a time, the opossum was rated as pretty nearly public enemy number one by certain groups of sportsmen. Now, however, there is greater understanding of the opossum and its foraging habits.

As previously stated, the opossum can and does eat everything, and an extensive examination of opossum scats or opossum stomachs will reveal every sort of material from horse meat to earthworms, and from oak leaves to grass roots. No one accuses the opossum of killing the horses or cutting down the oak trees, and probably most of the flesh is obtained from carcasses.

Opossums do catch chickens from small farms when they get into the roost at night and do rob birds' nests when they discover them, and will eat any young animal they can catch. But opossums are too slow, clumsy and stupid to make much of a living from active prey.

Fears that opossums would drive raccoons out of hollow trees and woodchucks from burrows have been pretty well disproved by investigations at wildlife research centers in the Midwest. Fears that opossums would multiply until they would become a menacing host have likewise proved groundless in the Midwest. The opossum simply cannot "take it" during a severe winter. He never learned to hibernate like the bear, raccoon, or woodchuck, and is obliged to get out and hustle for food if a storm lasts more than a day or two. When he gets out in near zero weather, he freezes his ears and his tail and often perishes from exposure. The opossum population in the Midwest always falls after a severe winter.

The opossum is of little economic importance in the Midwest. Although opossum is eagerly eaten in the south, it has never become popular in the north, and few trappers will skin an opossum for the price of the pelt.

The opossum does not appear to be a serious threat to any of our other wildlife species, but neither does he seem to be a particularly desirable addition to our native fauna. Anyway, he is here, and there doesn't seem to be anything we can do about it, so we may as well view him philosophically as an interesting example of a living fossil, going about his affairs, calmly unaware of the fact that he was born a million years too late.

Opossum
Didelphis virginiana

Size:	About that of a large housecat.
Range:	Throughout the Great Lakes although rarer further north.
Habitat:	Widely varied from meadows to forests and urban areas. Eats nuts, insects, reptiles, amphibians, uneaten dog food.
Fact:	The opossum has 50 teeth, more than any other mammal of the region.

Moles and Shrews--
Feisty Insectivores

The family *Soricidae*, to which the shrews belong, includes a number of species of small creatures, mostly even smaller than a mouse. In anatomy, they are as different to mice as a small badger is to a large gray rabbit. This difference would be easier to understand if we could get a mouse and a shrew side by side, and magnify each to the size of a dog or cat.

Actually, the skulls of a shrew and a mouse are as different as are the skulls of a tiger and a hippopotamus. The teeth of mice, like those of all rodents, consist of two upper and two lower incisors in front, then a wide toothless gap, and then a compact group of molar or grinding teeth in the rear of the mouth.

The teeth of a shrew, on the other hand, consist of 32 tiny sharp biting teeth, with no gap between them at all. The mouse is primarily a gnawer of roots and grains, while the shrew is almost exclusively a consumer of animal food. The mouse is a cowardly little fellow, always in fear for his life, while the shrew is a veritable little tiger, not afraid to face any odds and able to kill a mouse twice his size and weight.

The most striking peculiarity of a shrew is his apparent lack of eyes and ears, and his long, sharp pointed nose. Eyes and ears are both present, and shrews can both see and hear, their hearing especially being remarkably acute. Their sense of smell is very well developed also, and as they live in or very close to the earth at all times, smell and hearing are more important to them than sight.

It is customary to speak of shrews as insect eaters, but perhaps they should really be numbered among the carnivores or true flesh eaters. They will eat any sort of live animal eagerly, but their tiny size practically restricts them to an insect diet. They are extraordinarily fierce and ravenous little beasts, and may actually devour twice their own weight of flesh in 24 hours.

They are extraordinarily fierce and ravenous little beasts, and may actually devour twice their own weight of flesh in 24 hours.

Almost Independent of Weather

Shrews are easily able to overcome field mice much larger than themselves. Their ferocity and appetite are equally astonishing in so tiny a creature. This inordinate appetite has its disadvantages for shrews since they soon die of starvation if not fed. For this reason, it is necessary to feed shrews well if several are placed in a cage together; otherwise they will kill and eat each other.

The voice of the shrew is pitched at the upper limit of the human ear, and indeed many persons cannot hear it at all. There is good reason to believe that shrews have a considerable series of notes, even something like a song, probably of use to them at mating time. They also have scent glands on their sides and underparts, which are thought to be of use at that period. Apparently shrews breed and mate at any time of year. Their underground habits permit them to be almost independent of the weather. Some species of shrews burrow almost as extensively as moles; others live most of the time on the surface of the ground. Some shrews take to water readily, while others rarely go near the water. Since shrews do not hibernate in winter, and die so soon if not fed, it is hard to see how they can survive the winter in any numbers. This they must do, however, for shrews are common animals in this part of the country. They may find enough dormant insects and grubs to ride them over the hard times of winter.

Hawks, owls, cats, and weasels are the chief enemies of shrews. The flesh of shrews is very rank, and they are not usually eaten by these enemies after they are killed. The enemies probably mistake the shrews for mice. There are in the Great Lakes region six species of shrews, the masked shrew, the saddle-backed shrew, the water shrew, the pygmy shrew, the least shrew, and the short-tailed shrew. The most common of these is the short-tailed shrew, also called the mole-shrew. It is more mole-like in appearance and larger than other shrews, and burrows in the earth almost like a true mole. The other shrews are not easily identified at sight.

Moles Kill and Eat Mice

Moles belong the family *Talpidae*, characterized by an extreme degree of specialization for underground life.

Moles are like shrews in their soft, velvety fur, their apparent lack of eyes, ears, and neck, their scantily haired tails, and the general appearance of their teeth; but they differ in being much larger, and in having the front feet enormously developed for digging.

We have two species of moles in this region, the common garden or ground mole and the star-nosed mole. Although the star-nosed mole is common in swampy lands, it is probably the least-known animal in the state. Biologists often receive reports of a strange animal caught near a swamp or stream. Much of the time these animals prove to be the star-nosed mole. As a matter of fact, the locality in which the specimen was taken is probably well settled by star-nosed moles, but their small size and aquatic habits prevent them from being often seen or captured.

The star-nosed mole has the family characteristics typical of the moles, but also possesses a remarkable fringe of 22 fleshy feelers surrounding its nose, and its tail is longer than in other moles, being twice the length of the body. The tail is also curious in that it becomes very thick and red during breeding season, with a sharp constriction next to the body.

Probably the feelers serve as a delicate organ of touch in discovering worms and insects in the soil.

Probably the feelers serve as a delicate organ of touch in discovering worms and insects in the soil. The star-nosed mole prefers swimming to digging and prefers a mossy bog or a wet marsh to a dry upland. It is also sociable in its habits, unlike the other moles and shrews, and is often found living in colonies.

More Beneficial Than Detrimental

The common or garden mole is familiar

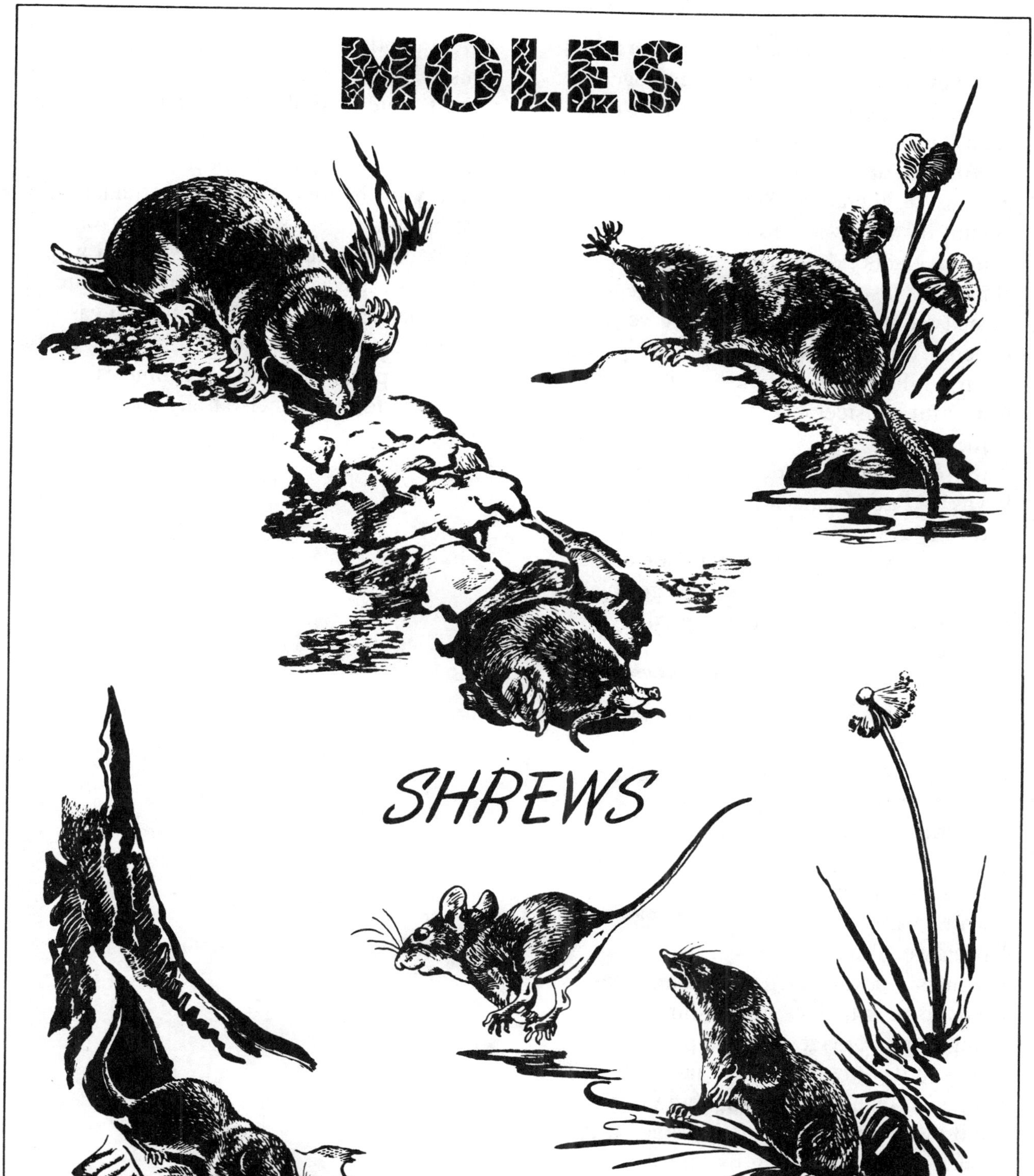
MOLES
SHREWS

to most people. Indeed, many persons think that they know the garden mole altogether too well, since they believe the moles do great damage to garden vegetables.

As a matter of fact, the moles caught in gardens are there because they are in pursuit of worms and insects, and not to damage plants. Moles and shrews live almost exclusively on animal food, and indeed are not fitted to eat coarse vegetable material. The numbers of mice and insects eaten by them should surely entitle them to respectful consideration by farmers and gardeners.

The real damage done by moles is to lawns and golf courses where their mounds and runways are decidedly a nuisance. It is true, however, that a mole will sometimes burrow the length of a row of vegetables, causing the roots to drop and partially destroying the row of plants.

The mole means well, for he is following the row in search of worms living among the roots, but like so many persons who "mean well," he becomes a pest himself, and sometimes needs to be killed to prevent him from doing more damage than the pests he is trying to destroy. Moles are far more beneficial than detrimental; shrews are almost 100 percent beneficial, since they do not damage anything by burrowing.

The mole means well, for he is following the row in search of worms living among the roots.

The strength of the mole is simply prodigious for an animal of its size, and the speed with which it moves through the ground is equally amazing. Its strength has been carefully estimated by tests in which the mole pushed aside weighted boxes on a floor, and the results showed that if a man were relatively as strong in proportion to his weight as a mole, he would have to exert a pressure of 12,000 pounds pushing against a weight.

Estimates have also been made of the ability of the mole to excavate tunnels and computation here shows that to perform a work equal to that of a mole, a man would have to excavate in a single night, a tunnel 37 miles long, and wide enough to easily permit the passage of his body. How lucky it is for prison wardens that inmates are not able to dig tunnels at any such rate as this!

Bats--
Mammalian Pursuit Planes

Bats are at once separated from all other mammals by their peculiar modification for flight. The forelimbs are much elongated, especially the fingers, and a thin, extensible membrane stretches over this framework, connecting also with the sides of the body and the hind legs. Another membrane stretches between the hind legs.

Besides their flying apparatus, bats are peculiar in having their hind legs twisted around in such a way that the knee bends backward. This makes it exceedingly difficult for them to walk, a mere flapping shuffle being the result of their utmost effort.

Bats are peculiar in having their hind legs twisted around in such a way that the knee bends backward.

On the wing, however, their movements are wonderfully graceful, and they turn and wheel in a manner not to be outdone by any bird. Other structures characteristic of bats are the peculiar leaf-like appendages to the nose, and the elongated lobe of the ear. In their general anatomy and their teeth, bats are rather closely related to the *Insectivora*--the moles and shrews. They are generally regarded, in fact, as a specialized offshoot from the insectivorous group.

Bats are widely distributed in all parts of the world, and vary in size from small species no larger than a house mouse to the big "flying foxes" of Malaysia, the expanded wings of which measure 30 inches or more from tip to tip. These large bats and their allies are fruit eaters, but most bats, including those of the United States, are insect eaters, and feed on the wing.

Some Species Migrate

Bats are nocturnal in habits and are most active at dusk and early in the morning, just before dawn. The daylight hours they spend at rest, hanging head downward by their hind feet, in some dark cave, building, or hollow tree. In winter, many bats hibernate in similar quarters, but there is also a southward migration of some species, like that of birds. The voice of bats is remarkably high-pitched and squeaky, and is heard when the bats are caught or disturbed while at rest in the daytime.

There are eight common species of bats in the Great Lakes region, all of which are fairly well distributed, especially in the southern part. All of these bats should be protected, since they are great destroyers of insects, and do no damage of any consequence.

Possibly the most common of Great Lakes bats is the little brown bat, which has a length of about three and a half inches, and a wing spread of about nine inches. Their flight is very swift and erratic, with such lightning-like zigzags as to be almost impossible to follow. The little brown bats are known to eat a large number of mosquitoes, which alone should endear them to humans.

A second species of Great Lakes bat, the keen bat, is not so plentiful as the little brown bat, and cannot be distinguished from this bat in flight. The principal difference is in the ears. The ears of the keen bat are very long, so that when laid forward they reach beyond the tip of the nose. The ears of the little brown bat are much shorter. The two bats are very similar in habits and flight.

Another species, the Indiana bat, differs from the little brown bat and the keen bat only in a few minor details.

The silvery bat is a little larger than the three species just named, and is a darker brown in color, frosted with whitish, from whence it received its name of silvery bat. It is less often seen than the foregoing bats, as it lives mostly along rivers and near the edge of open woods. It nests commonly in hollow trees. In flight, it is not quite so swift and erratic as are the other three species.

Great Lakes Bat Are Harmless

Another common Great Lakes bat is the big brown bat. This bat is considerably larger than the bats already described, and does not usually appear quite so early in the evening. It also flies a little closer to the ground than is customary with these bats.

They are able to bite sharply if handled carelessly, but are certainly less dangerous than a rat, or even a full-grown mouse.

The big brown bat often enters houses, and sometimes frightens persons who awake to see a creature whose size is exaggerated in the darkness flying silently about the room. However, all Great Lakes bats are absolutely harmless, and need not be feared in any way. They are able to bite sharply if handled carelessly, but are certainly less dangerous than a rat, or even a full-grown mouse.

The evening bat is much like the big brown bat, but considerably smaller.

The red bat is less common in the Great Lakes states than the previous species, but still is often seen. It comes out earliest of all in the evening, and in fact may sometimes be seen while it is light, in which case its bright red color serves as a distinguishing identification mark. This bat normally spends the day hanging alone in a tree. A female might be found hanging with her one to four young clinging to her.

The hoary bat is our largest Great Lakes bat, but is less common than any of the other species. These bats appear only after darkness has set in, so that they are barely distinguishable against the sky. The large-size wingspread of about 15 inches, the sharp, narrow wings, and the marvelous rapidity of flight serve to identify the hoary bat. The color is brownish, frosted with whitish, from whence comes the name hoary bat. These bats seem to be migratory, and are found in the southern states during the winter months.

The female bat carries the young about with her on her nightly flights, the little bats clinging tightly to the hair of the mother's body. This habit is necessary with bats, since they make no nest of any sort. The presence of the young, which number from one to three, does not seem to impede the flight of the mother to any noticeable extent. The young seem to be able to care for themselves after about 50

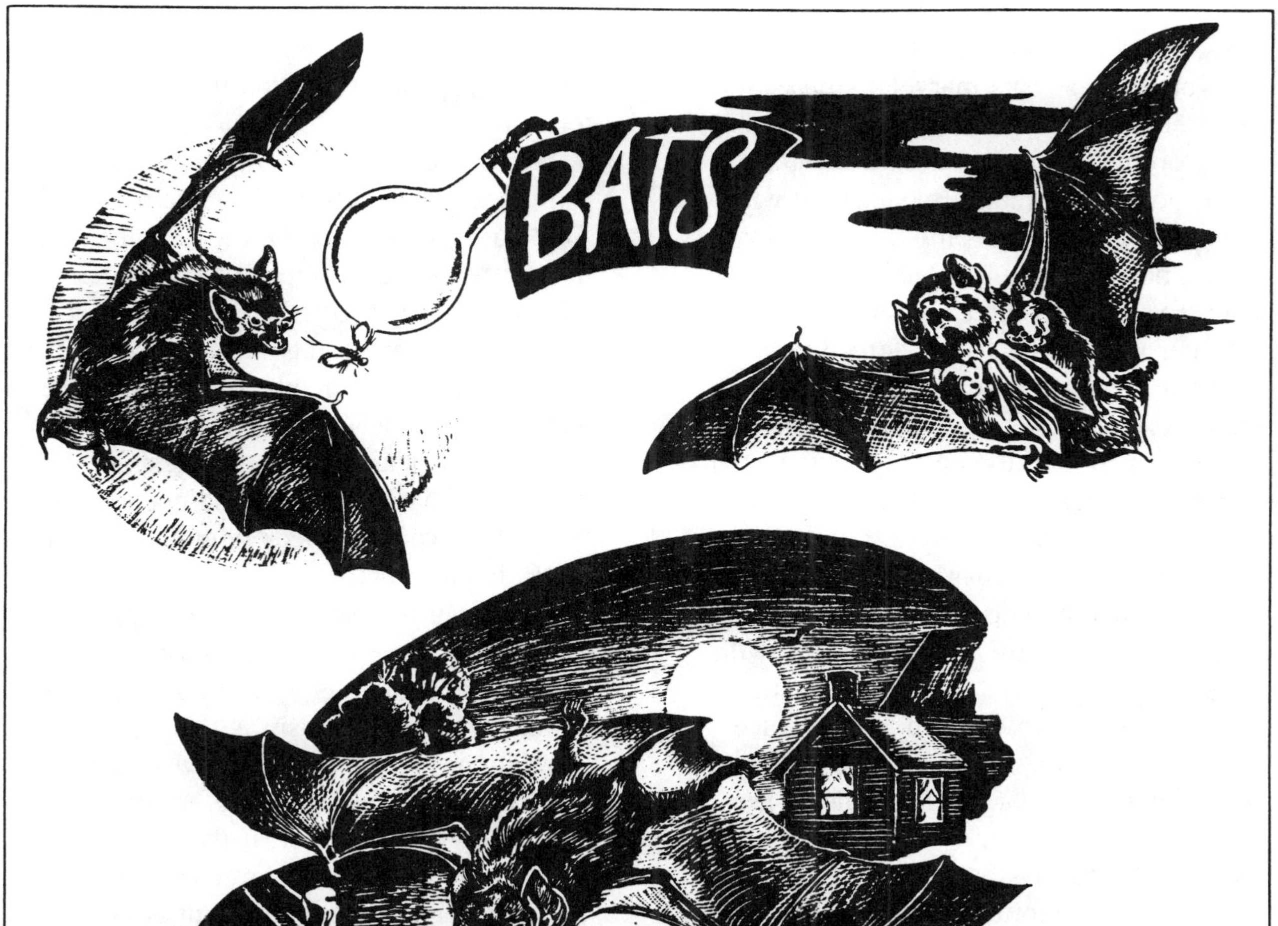
BATS

days; just shy of two months.

Not only are bats marvelous fliers, unexcelled by any bird, they are also able to fly around obstructions in a manner even more remarkable. Bats can fly with great speed about a room which is hung with a network of wires, never touching a wire. Even silken threads hung so close together that the bats were forced to contract their wings to pass between them were avoided perfectly for hours at a time.

Studies around the country have shown that bats navigate and hunt their food by use of an echo-location system much more discriminating than man's invention of sonar. Researchers used a high-speed electronic flash camera synchronized with a super-high-fidelity tape recorder. The bats were found to emit up to 200 voice beeps per second, detecting the returning echoes with their large ears. Able to hear an echo from a target as tiny as a mosquito, a bat has been observed by means of slow motion films to catch two fruit flies in a half second, as many as 220 in 15 minutes!

Bat Guano Is Valuable

While in the Great Lakes region, as in most states, bats have little or no economic importance aside from their destruction of insects, there are places where they are worth a good deal of money. This is due to the great number of bats which roost in some caves where their droppings accumulate to form deposits of guano.

Perhaps the best-known example is in Carlsbad Cavern, New Mexico. Carlsbad Cavern, the largest cave yet discovered, was located by following the immense flight of bats which emerged each evening and spread over the surrounding region. So tremendous is the number of bats roosting in the cavern that their flight can be seen for miles, and a roaring mass of bats emerges near dusk like the funnel of a tornado.

From one to five million bats are estimated to come from the cavern at dusk. That number has dwindled in recent years due to the widespread use of pesticides, which kills the insects bats depend upon for food. The enormous guano deposits in the cave reached a depth of a hundred feet, and extended for a quarter of a mile. Between 1901 and 1921, thousands of carloads of bat guano were shipped from the great cavern at prices ranging from 20 to 40 dollars per ton.

Although the bats at Carlsbad emerge through the same entrance used by human visitors, their roost is in a different part of the cavern. Also, tourism is managed by the National Park Service to avoid conflicts with the bat population there. Many people, however, wait near the cavern entrance to see the extraordinary spectacle of the bat "tornado" roaring out at dusk.

The Black Bear--
Buffoon of the North Woods

Bears have always excited the interest of humans, and have perhaps given rise to more legends and anecdotes than have any other mammal. While lions, tigers, or elephants may be more spectacular in some respects, their habitat lies in distant lands, and their contact with European and American civilization has been much less than that of the bears, who inhabit the northern portion of the earth.

Legends and stories about bears abound in the literature of our European ancestry with fact and fancy so interwoven that it is difficult to reconstruct any clear picture of the true relationship between man and bear in earlier times. It is evident from the stories, however, that bears appeared far more formidable to men armed with spears or bows than to men armed with guns, and that the animals themselves were far bolder and more dangerous than they seem nowadays.

Family Peculiarities

Bears are massive, clumsy beasts, with thick limbs, big, strongly clawed, plantigrade, naked soled feet, and an ability to take the world as they find it. It is in the skull and teeth that bears differ most from other carnivores.

The teeth have a general resemblance to those of dogs, but the broad, flat molars are better adapted to grinding than cutting, and the flesh teeth are more massive and blunt. Other family peculiarities are the extreme shortness of tail, the coarse body hair, and the habit of standing erect to feed or to look around. Perhaps this habit of standing erect, like a clumsy caricature of a man, is what makes the bear a symbol of buffoonery. Bears are comical creatures in captivity, and are often comical in the wild as well, to the few persons fortunate enough to observe them in their natural habitat.

Bears are rather solitary, the males wandering about alone, the females accompanied by cubs as big as themselves. The young, usually two, but sometimes one, three, or four, are born during the winter while the female is in the den, which may be a rocky cave or the hollow of an old tree, the middle of a dense thicket, or merely a bed beneath the snow.

Born Naked and Blind

The cubs are surprisingly small at birth, being about eight inches long, and weighing from nine to 12 ounces. This is about 1/200 to 1/250 of the mother's weight, while a deer fawn weighs 1/30, a puppy 1/25, a human baby 1/20, and a young porcupine 1/15 of the average mother's weight. A newborn porcupine is actually larger and heavier than a newborn black bear.

The cubs are born naked and blind, and develop slowly.

The cubs are born naked and blind, and develop slowly; hence the mother is extremely attentive about them, and recklessly brave in their defense. Most recorded instances of unprovoked attacks by bears have been cases of mothers who saw or fancied their babies in danger.

Most of the smaller birds and mammals keep out of their reach.

Although bears are big, powerful and courageous, their weight and their dislike of violent exertion prevent them from preying upon the large grazers such as moose, elk, and deer. Most of the smaller birds and mammals keep out of their reach. The flesh black bears eat is chiefly that of animals too young to escape, or such as they take through accidental good luck.

Carrion is another important source of meat, and when a large carcass is found bears are likely to scrape a shallow pit nearby and half bury, half cover it over for future use. Fish are greatly appreciated by all bears and may form the principal source of food for some of the far northern species. Black bears take fish when they can get them, but fish are only incidental in their diets.

Diet is Mostly Vegetarian

Black bears are industrious hunters of small mammals such as mice, voles, spermophiles, and chipmunks, and manage to dig out a good many of these animals from day to day. If their digging out of little creatures seems small business for big bears, still more ridiculous is the fact that insects form an important part of their diet. The insects most sought for are those which dwell in colonies or have nests stored with luscious grubs or honey.

All over the world, bears' favorite summer occupation is tearing rotten logs and stumps to pieces in search of fat larvae, and digging out ants and bees from their nests in the ground or in tree trunks. The outraged bees swarm over the marauder, creep into his coat, eyes, ears, and mouth, stinging him until he rolls on the ground and roars in a fury of pain, daubing his eyes and ears with dirt and honey as he tries to brush off his tormentors.

But the bears' appetite outlasts his distress.

But the bears' appetite outlasts his distress and he keeps at it until gorged, cloyed, and smeared with honey. He stumbles off to some retreat where he can sleepily but delightedly lick off his fur and digest his meal.

Despite his fondness for all types of meat, from carrion to ants, bears subsist largely on vegetable fare, because he is usually physically incapable of getting enough meat. Fruit, berries, roots, bark, lichens, tender shoots, leaves--all are eaten when and where available. When nuts and berries are ripe in the fall, the bear eats and grows fat. With the onset of cold weather, he become extremely fat, picks out a secluded spot, and turns in for the winter.

Hibernation

The hibernation of the bear seems to be a matter of necessity, depending upon climate and ability to get food. In very cold and snowy countries, bears den up early and may be snowed under for many weeks. They do not become torpid like

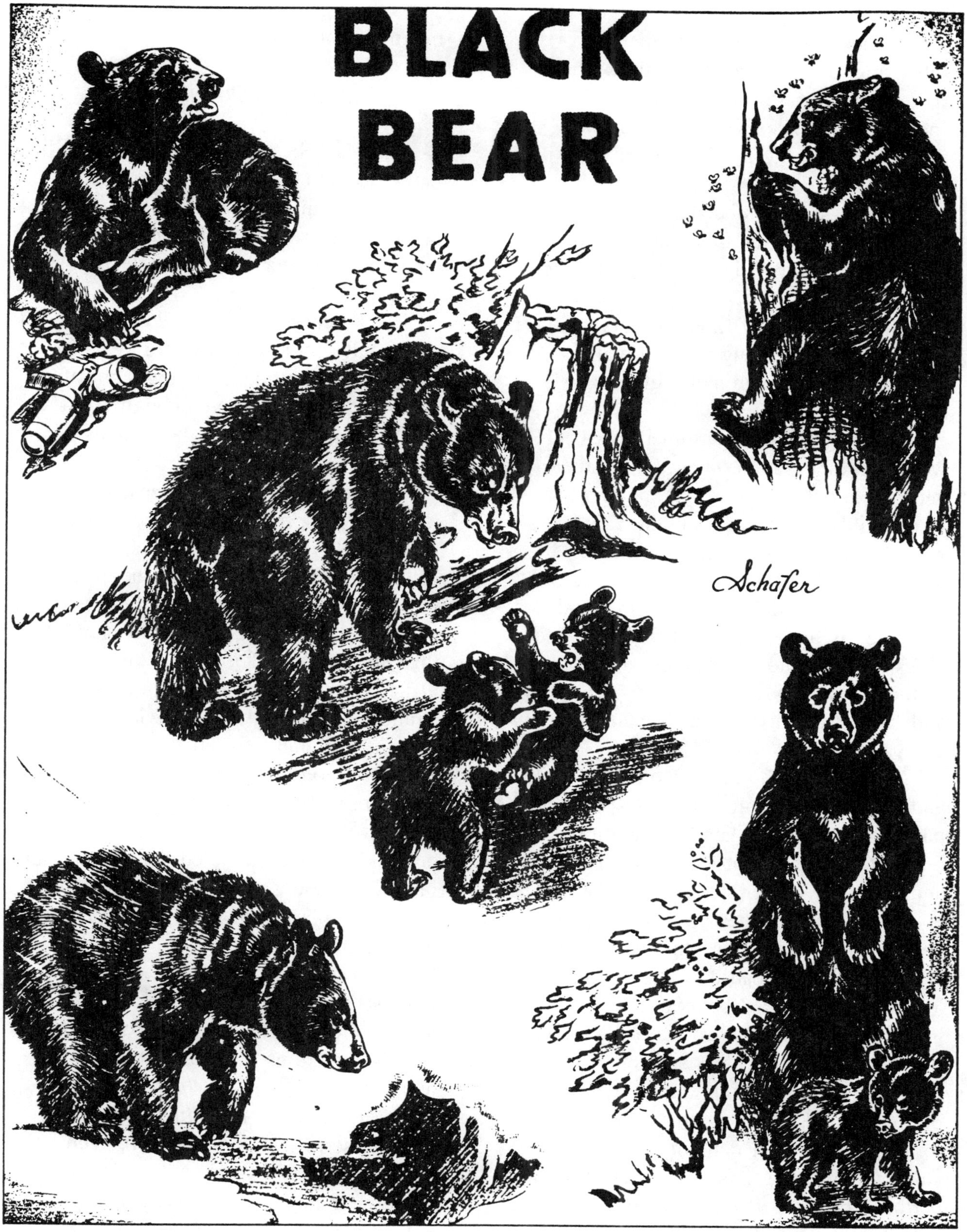
BLACK
BEAR
Schafer

woodchucks, but simply lie quietly, subsisting on their accumulated fat, the slow assimilation of which sustains life and enables the females to nurse their cubs, which are born during this winter retirement.

There has always been much speculation about the hibernation of bears, and accurate knowledge has been hard to get until recent years. A study of wild bears requires lots of time and lots of space, since bears range over a wide territory, and are extremely difficult to observe.

It has always been assumed that bears went into hibernation when the weather became so cold or the snow so deep that food could no longer be obtained. Yet it was also known that bears sometimes disappeared from an area suddenly before cold weather or deep snow set in. Evidence has recently appeared which indicates that bears may go into hibernation, not because of the weather, but because they get so fat and their stomachs so full that they literally can eat no more.

At this time, the bear's stomach shrinks, and the animal apparently is incapable of taking more food. When this condition is reached, the bear hunts up a suitable spot, and starts his winter sleep. Now, the question remains, does the bear quit eating because his stomach has shrunk or does his stomach shrink because he quit eating? At least, it appears, that bears begin hibernation after they are "fed up," rather than when food becomes scarce.

Using radio-tracking collars, wildlife biologists and other scientists are now able to locate the winter dens of bears and study them during this most interesting period. They hope to learn more about breeding as well as how the kidneys and other organs function during hibernation. The results could improve medical treatment for humans.

Holding His Own in Numbers

The black bear, the only species of bear native to the Great Lakes region, is maintaining in numbers throughout its range and there is recent evidence that its range may be increasing slightly from north to south.

Black bears are adept at keeping out of sight, and people may live for years in bear country without catching sight of one. A single bear may leave enough "sign" to give the impression that the "woods are full of bears."

Overturned logs and stones, stumps torn to pieces, bushes trampled down, limbs torn off low trees, and perhaps tons of earth scattered about may merely indicate that one hungry bear has been trying to satisfy his appetite. In view of this abundance of "bear sign" and the difficulty of seeing even one bear, it is not strange that dependable knowledge of bears is so scarce, and that much of the traditional lore is of doubtful authenticity.

To most hunters, a bear is the highest prize of the hunting season, even outranking a well-antlered deer. While an individual bear does occasionally damage orchards, apiaries, or farm stock, bears in general are harmless to man's interests, and their value as top notch tourist attractions and hunting trophies entitle them to serious consideration among our most valued natural resources.

To most hunters, a bear is the highest prize of the hunting season, even outranking a well-antlered deer.

Conflicts with Humans

Since many small dumps were closed for environmental concerns, the number of bear-human conflicts has dropped considerably. It is no longer entertainment in the country to go to the dump and feed the bears.

A study of wild bears requires lots of time and lots of space.

But black bears have attacked humans, although such attacks are extremely rare. Bears have learned that backpackers can be "bluffed" into giving up their packs and running, leaving an easy meal for the bear. The best course of action is to stand your ground and make lots of noise.

If a bear stubbornly comes too close, it is better to lose a backpack than take a chance. Some hikers carry pepper spray, which has proven in most cases to dissuade bears from bothering humans.

Another way to avoid conflicts with bears is to keep food contained and inaccessible.

Black Bear
Ursus americanus

Size: 240-500 pounds
Range: Northern Great Lakes region.
Habitat: Forests, both upland and swampy. Eats mainly vegetative matter such as roots and berries but also grubs and other insects found in rotten stumps and logs.
Fact: Black bears live up to 13 years in the wild and generally avoid contact with humans.

Raccoons--
Masked Clowns of the Woodlots

Captain John Smith, in his report on Virginia, mentions "a beast they call the aroughcun, much like a badger, but useth to lie in trees as squirrels doe."

The early Americans soon shortened these sonorous syllables to "raccoon" and then cut even that down to "coon." If we were to dock his tail, and not look too closely at his face, the raccoon is "much like a badger" as the observant Smith said. But this superficial likeness is soon forgotten, for the masked face, flexible nose, flat-soled feet, arched hindquarters, and long, ringed tail are quite different from badger characteristics. And, of course, the raccoon is a climber and the badger a digger.

Is Primarily a Woodsman

The home of a raccoon family is usually in a hollow tree where a limb has broken off or a trunk hole has rotted large enough for their accommodations. But now and then a place is selected on or near the ground, like a hollow log, or even in some cases a tile drain or a woodchuck hole. However, the raccoon is primarily a woodsman, and rather prefers swampy woods.

In the raccoon's chosen retreat, the young are produced, usually in April and May in the Great Lakes region. The gestation period is about 63 days, and the average per litter is about four.

The young are ready to leave the den at about ten weeks of age. Raccoons do not hibernate in the strict sense of the word, but "den up" most of the winter, becoming active upon the slightest disturbance, or whenever mild weather comes along. Deep snow seems to be the chief factor causing raccoons to den up. As raccoons have become more plentiful a lone animal is seen now and then in the daytime, scared up by a hunter's dog or stretched out on a big limb or curled up in a tree crotch lazily enjoying a sunbath.

Raccoon is Omnivorous

The raccoon is, like man, omnivorous; that is, he eats pretty nearly everything that comes along, and is not restricted to either a meat or vegetable diet. He eats flesh of any kind, including small birds and mammals when he can catch them, and sometimes gets into trouble in the farmers poultry yard.

He devours eggs eagerly, and digs up turtle eggs along the shores of lakes and streams. He is particularly fond of fish, and displays considerable dexterity in capturing them with his forepaws.

He is particularly fond of fish.

He is also a most successful frog hunter and may be tracked in the mud along creek banks, where he catches and eats frogs, snails, crayfish, mussels, etc. Inspects are eaten when available, as are slugs and snails. Various vegetable products are included in the diet at all seasons.

Research reveals that acorns are eaten very extensively by raccoons during nearly all times of the year, even in winter. Grapes and other available fruits are eaten during the fall.

Raccoons are notoriously near-sighted and their poor vision likely limits the amount of prey they can catch. What they lack in keen eyesight in made up for in curiosity, however, and much food is found by chance.

The raccoon is as clever as a monkey with his paws, and the sight of one sitting with his back against a log, holding something to eat between his hind feet, while daintily picking away and handing morsels to his mouth with his fore paws, is irresistibly comic. Give him part of a loaf of bread, and he will first of all dig a deep hole down into it, now and then cocking up a knowing eye as if to ask what you think of his method.

One of the singular peculiarities of the raccoon is his habit of dipping his food in water, or washing it, to which he owes his specific name of *lotor*, the washer. Various explanations of this have been advanced, but probably the simplest--that it wants to clean the food--is nearest to the truth. Bears do somewhat the same thing on occasion, and often soak hard bread and other dry, stiff food before eating it.

Raccoons Insist on Privacy

Another peculiarity of the raccoon is his insistence of privacy, as demonstrated in wild observations. Ring-tails have left den trees to establish new homes, when temperatures have hovered near the zero point and snow has been two feet deep in the woods, after researchers have approached the dens close enough to allow the raccoons to catch a sniff of the intruders. In one instance, a female raccoon took her family from a den so situated that she had to go through flooded waters to get to a new location.

It seems evident that the woodlot which is left undisturbed is apt to have a greater number of raccoons than the one in which hollow trees are molested.

It seems evident that the woodlot which is left undisturbed is apt to have a greater number of raccoons than the one in which hollow trees are molested.

The world's prize delicacy in the raccoon's opinion is sweet corn, when in the milky condition of sweetness which so attracts squirrels, mice, birds (and you and me). He strips back the husk neatly and disposes of the soft kernels with ease and dispatch. This is his chief occupation on the still, hot nights of late August and early September. It is at this time that he is at his fattest and largest, and that his flesh is sweetest and best flavored.

A young raccoon, fattened on corn in the milk is considered one of nature's choicest tidbits by those who have tried it. In winter and spring, raccoon meat is rather poor provender, but in late summer and fall it is highly esteemed in many parts of the United States, and was presumably the original stimulus for the famous American sport of raccoon hunting. Raccoon hunting is truly an American sport, since these animals do not occur in

RACCOON

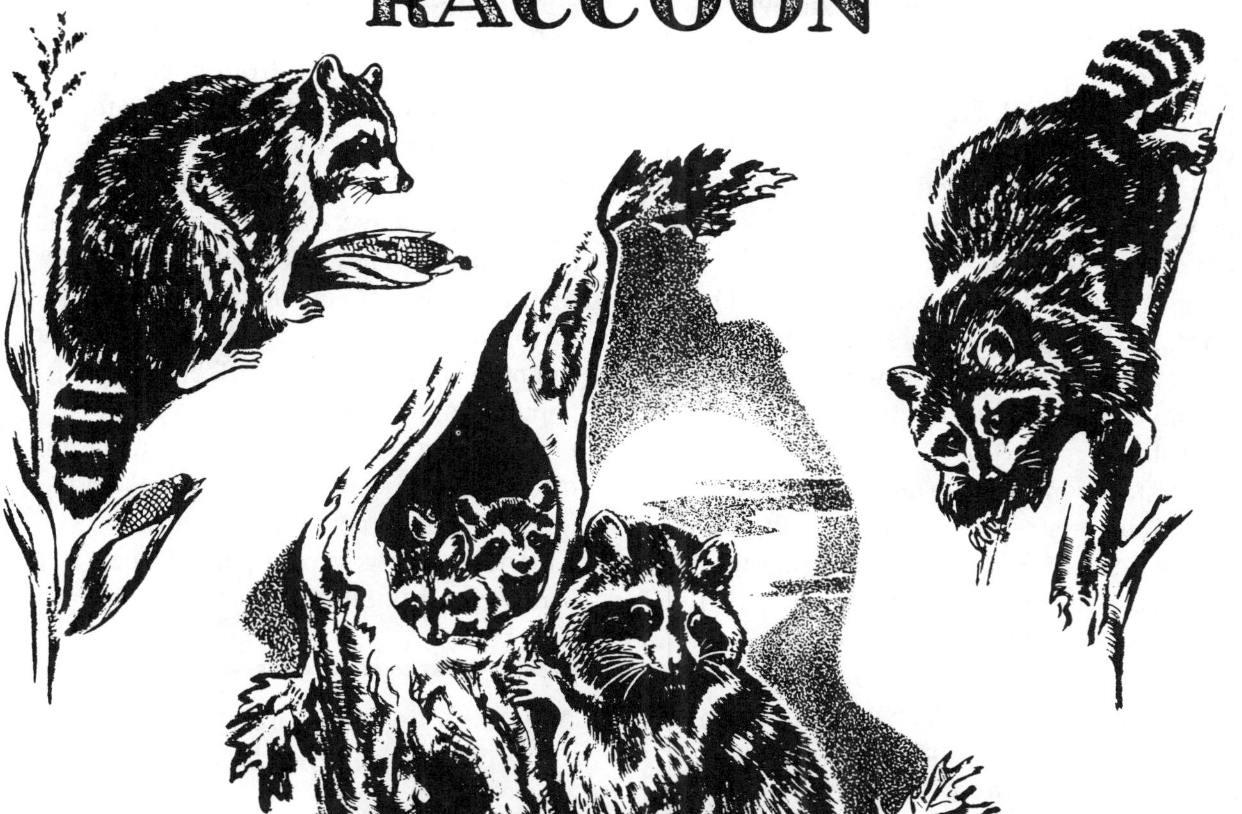

other parts of the world.

It is, in truth, a comical sort of hunting, yet it calls for a lot of endurance, since an old raccoon may run four or five miles after he has started, zigzagging hither and yon, circling around and around trees, leaving a track calculated to make a dog dizzy, swimming streams, and running along the tops of logs and rail fences, hiding his trail with the craft of a fox. One either goes for it or he doesn't, but a dyed-in-the-wool raccoon hunter won't admit that any other form of hunting can quite equal it.

The raccoon is important as a fur bearer, but it is regarded more highly as a game animal by hunters, and the present trend seems to be toward hunting raccoon for sport, rather than merely for fur.

The relatively low price of raccoon pelts in recent years as compared to many other furs has perhaps had considerable influence in this way. However, there are trappers who take the animals for fur alone, and it is difficult to establish satisfactory regulations because of these conflicting interests. To the hunter, whose enjoyment of the chase is paramount, primeness of the fur is of secondary importance, while to the trapper, primeness of the fur is of primary importance.

Have Increased in Numbers

No longer are raccoons the curiosity they were a generation ago to rural and city folk alike. Since the late 1940's they have become very plentiful and numerous reports and complaints are received by state wildlife officials of raccoons setting up housekeeping in barns and other out-buildings. They have even been found in storerooms and attics of city stores.

When opossums first became abundant in the region years ago, many persons were seriously concerned lest the newcomer drive out the raccoon. This fear seems not to have been well founded, since opossums have suffered severely from population fluctuations, mainly because of winter weather too severe for them, while raccoons have gained consistently.

Raccoons have adapted well to human development. They consume uneaten dog food and garbage left in suburban yards. Unfortunately, they are also susceptible to canine distemper, which affects their population periodically.

Certainly no one would like to see the raccoon disappear from our woods and fields, for he is peculiarly a native American, and is a vital part of our heritage and tradition.

Raccoon
Procyon lotor

Size:	13-44 pounds
Range:	Throughout the Great Lakes Region in both urban and rural settings although woodlots are preferred.
Habitat:	Prefers wooded areas but will thrive in urban areas where there are hollow places for denning.
Fact:	The raccoon's mask camouflages its small, black eyes if attacked. It can be a fierce fighter.

The Weasel--
Nemesis of Nature's Little Ones

Slender, lithe, sharp of tooth and claw, secretively colored, richly endowed with strength, speed, cleverness, and indomitable courage, weasels are the scourge of all small ground-living animals.

There are several species of weasels--three in the Great Lakes region--which differ somewhat in size, length of tail, and other minor characteristics, but all are similar in food habits, ferocity, and manner of life, so that a single description will suffice for all.

The cunning savagery of the weasel is reflected in his physical appearance, which at times is peculiarly ferocious. The forehead is low, and the nose sharp; the eyes are small, penetrating, cunning, and seem to glitter with a baleful green light. The jaws are worked by muscles which cover the whole side of the skull. This face is set on a long, slender neck in such a way that it can be held at a right angle with the neck axis.

The cunning savagery of the weasel is reflected in his physical appearance.

When we suddenly come upon a weasel, its neck stretched up, flat triangular head swaying from one side to the other, little beady eyes gleaming, we are reminded that ounce for ounce, he's one of the greatest little fighters in North America.

Kills More Than He Can Eat

The weasel preys on every living creature which he can catch and kill, and this includes pretty nearly everything from a turkey to a sparrow, and from a rabbit to a shrew. Swift and surefooted, he pursues and runs down his prey; keen of scent, he tracks them; slim and sinuous he follows them into their burrows, and in the end kills them even in their secret nests. Perhaps he does not kill for the sheer love of killing as some allege, but at least his desire to kill sometimes seems to get the better of him, and he kills far more than he can possibly eat.

We should not too bitterly condemn him for this: he is merely "accumulating a surplus for a possible period of future scarcity," as economists describe similar actions among our own species.

When a weasel finds himself in the presence of a number of creatures which he considers his natural prey as, for example, in a poultry yard, or a mouse nest, he cannot restrain his fierce desires, but kills them all. This wholesale destruction we view with horror in the poultry yard and with delight in the mouse nest. The weasel is perhaps the most efficient destroyer of small rodents known.

He kills them by day and by night, in their snug retreats and in the open, in all seasons of the year.

The weasel's killing seems to be regulated only by the scarcity or abundance of prey, and by the limitations of time and space. Yet regulated, it must be, for the creatures never multiply until we have a plague of weasels, nor do they ever exterminate their prey over any considerable area. Occasionally a weasel or a weasel family will settle in an old barn teeming with rats and remain until not a rat can be found. But even here rats reappear after the weasels have gone, so extermination is not quite accomplished.

The weasel's killing seems to be regulated only by the scarcity or abundance of prey.

Is Efficient "Control Agent"

The law of diminishing returns operates in nature as well as in the realm of human economics, and when one type of prey becomes scarce, more attention is turned to other types. Hence, the weasel is one of the most efficient agents in maintaining the much-discussed "balance of nature," since he tends to control certain species without exterminating them.

It is generally conceded that weasels do more good than harm from a human viewpoint, since the occasional raid on the poultry yard or the occasional killing of a rabbit, grouse or pheasant is more than offset by the incessant destruction of mice, rats, and other small rodents, which are important pests in agricultural areas.

A characteristic of the weasel is his habit of storing food supplies. This is the more surprising since the weasel craves fresh hot blood from living prey, and seldom, if ever, eats from its storage pile of carcasses. Yet a weasel has been known to accumulate as many as a hundred carcasses of mice or rats dragging some of them a considerable distance to augment the heap.

It is not often realized that weasels can climb trees, but they climb easily and rapidly, and are said to catch chipmunks in that way, although red squirrels easily elude them.

Even larger squirrels may at times be caught in their tree dens, although squirrel catching seems the exception rather than the rule. Unlike his larger cousin, the mink, the weasel is not an expert swimmer, and does not pursue aquatic prey.

Observations on the family life of the weasel are scarce, and our knowledge of the subject is, therefore, limited. The gestation period of the long-tailed weasel, our most common species in the region, is apparently about 130 days, and five to eight young are born in late April or early May.

The male is believed to remain with the family for a time and to assist in gathering food for them. The nest may be in a hollow log, a stone pile, or under an old barn or brushpile, and usually shows remains of mice or other prey along with the grass and hair of the original construction. The young leave the nest at about six weeks of age, and wander with the mother for the remainder of the summer. They seem to become solitary during the fall and early winter, pairing off some time in mid-winter.

Observations on the family life of the weasel are scarce, and our knowledge of the subject is, therefore, limited.

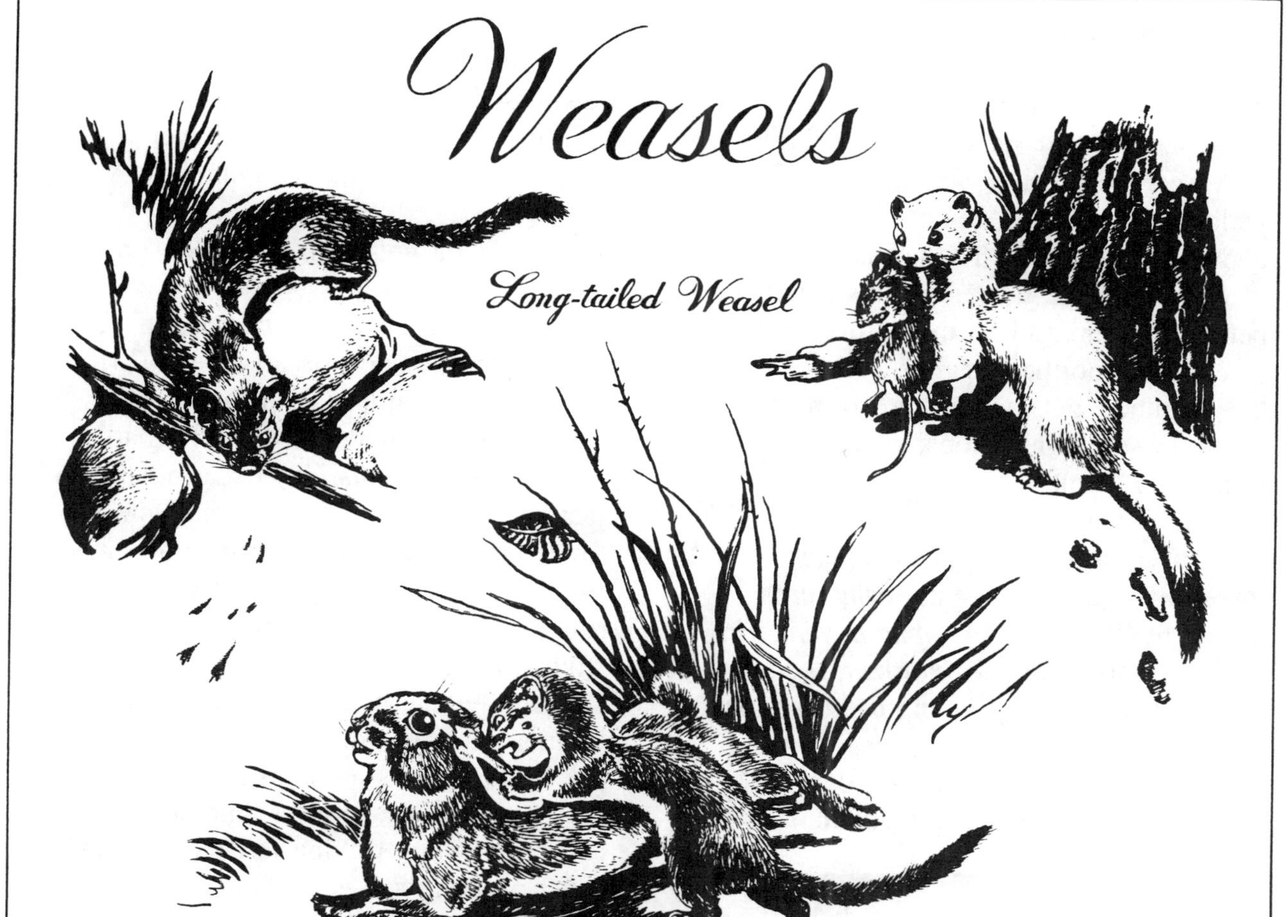
Weasels
Long-tailed Weasel
Schafer
Short-tailed Weasel
Least Weasel

The long-tailed weasel, also called the New York weasel, is the largest as well as the most abundant species in this region. Its upper parts are dark brown, while its under parts are white, washed with dull yellow. The white does not usually continue on the feet. The tail is tipped with black in both the winter and the summer pelage. This weasel normally turns white in winter in northern region, and becomes the "ermine," but may not do so in the south. In southern regions, some weasels turn white, some remain brown, and some become mixed in color during the winter.

This weasel normally turns white in winter in northern region, and becomes the "ermine," but may not do so in the south.

The short-tailed or Bonaparte, weasel is somewhat smaller than the long-tailed weasel, but is quite similar in color, except that the feet and toes usually show white. The tail is much shorter than that of the long-tailed weasel, which together with the white on the feet, enables the observer to readily separate the two species.

A third species, the least weasel, is little known and seldom seen by Great Lakes residents, yet it is probably found in all parts of the region. This weasel, smallest of our carnivores, is only about six to seven inches long, including the short tail. The body is about the thickness of a man's thumb.

General coloration and color changes are like that of the other species, but the tail is not tipped with black in either color phase. Food habits are thought to be similar to other weasels, but the small size probably restricts the diet to mice, insects, and possibly small birds. While records of these little weasels are few, it is believed that they are often taken by trappers and dismissed as "young weasels" without further ado, as their tiny pelts would scarcely be worth the skinning.

Fairly Abundant in the Region

Since weasels are so fierce, active, and adaptable, the question arises as to why they do not multiply until they destroy their own livelihood by devouring all available prey. This may occasionally actually occur in a limited area, where mice and other small mammals become reduced to such a degree that weasels must migrate or starve. It is known that bloody fights between individual weasels frequently take place, and the vanquished animal often lies dead on the battlefield.

Male weasels are considerably larger and heavier than females, and since these males are quite lacking in chivalry outside of the mating and early family period, a losing fight for the female means no family thereafter. This may constitute a ruthless but effective check on weasel multiplication.

In addition to this, weasels are known to suffer from various diseases which affect mink, so disease may also play a part in controlling their numbers.

Weasels are fairly abundant in the Great Lakes region, but few trappers or hunters make any direct attempts to take them, and those taken are shot or trapped incidentally to other activities.

Short-Tailed Weasel (~~Ermine~~)
Mustela erminea

Size: 2 to 5.5 ounces
Range: Most of the Great Lakes region although generally not found in Illinois and Indiana.
Habitat: Prefers a variety of habitats including woodlands and open forests near streams.
Fact: Most live only 1 to 2 years in the wild.

Long-Tailed Weasel
Mustela frenata

Size: 3 to 9.5 ounces
Range: Most of the Great Lakes region except parts of Ontario.
Habitat: Prefers edges of woodlots and brushlands.
Fact: Wraps its body around victims to prevent escape and kills with a quick bite to the base of the skull.

Least Weasel
Mustela nivalis

Size: 1 to 2 ounces
Range: Most of the Great Lakes region except Michigan's Upper Peninsula and parts of Ontario.
Habitat: Prefers edges of woodlots and brushlands. Uses a variety of habitats.
Fact: The least weasel hunts day and night for food.

The Mink--
Jack of all Trades

The mink is one of the best-known and most important members of the weasel family--the *Mustelidae*. Mink are very much like big weasels; but somewhat heavier in build.

Wild mink are nearly uniform umber brown, darker and glossier on the back, and deepening to black on the tail. The chin is more or less white with some white spots frequently appearing on the throat, breast, or belly. Through intensive breeding, a wide variety of color phases have been developed in captive mink. Unlike weasels, mink do not turn white in winter.

> ***The mink is widely distributed over the North American continent, regardless of civilization.***

The mink is widely distributed over the North American continent, regardless of civilization, which interferes little, if at all, with its ability to make a living. Alaskan and Pacific coast examples are larger and darker, while those of the Gulf states are lighter both in color and weight than those of the interior and North Atlantic states. Mink are also found in northern Europe and Siberia.

Fur is Valuable Resource

The fur of all northern mink is of great beauty and value when taken during the cold months, and the trapping of mink not only engages the attention of professional trappers, but puts many a dollar into the pockets of farmers and farmers' sons all over the country. Ranch-grown mink produce a large percentage of all mink coats, stoles, and neck pieces.

The mink is easily the most versatile member of the weasel family. A family is largely composed of specialists. For example, the weasel is specialized for catching small prey on the ground, the marten is specialized for catching prey in trees, the badger for digging prey out of the ground, the otter for catching prey in the water, and the skunk is highly specialized for defending himself while wandering about looking for prey in the open.

The mink, however, can catch fish and amphibians in the water, mice and ground squirrels on the land, or squirrels in their leafy homes, with equal celerity. True, like most jacks of all trades, he is not quite as good at any particular trade as is the true specialist, but he can make a living almost anywhere. He cannot swim as well as the otter, climb as well as the marten, catch mice as well as the weasel, dig as well as the badger, or smell as bad as the skunk, be he can do a credible job at each of those tasks.

Active Chiefly at Night

The mink is endowed with boundless resources in the face of danger as well as in the matter of getting a living. Wander where he will, day or night, it is of small consequence whether the enemy that attacks him is fox, dog, wildcat, otter, hawk, or owl, he is always within a couple of jumps of some place of refuge. If water is near, he dives without a splash and slides away like a fish, almost as much at home as the fish themselves in the swirling eddies and dim passages beneath sunken logs and driftwood. They come to the surface here and there for breath until the enemy is left hopelessly behind.

When water is not close at hand, he can go up the nearest tree like a squirrel, or dart into any hole or crevice that would hide a rat; and if no natural retreat whatever is available, he can outrun and outdodge any ordinary pursuer. If finally cornered, he is so quick and savage a fighter as to stand a chance against a foe much larger than himself.

The mink is active chiefly by night, and most of his hunting occurs at that time. However, mink are frequently observed hunting or traveling in broad daylight, and seem equally at home whether under the noonday sun or the midnight moon.

The mink is active chiefly by night, and most of his hunting occurs at that time.

Is Both Hero and Villain

As might be expected of a predatory animal so adaptable and physically capable as the mink, his diet is widely varied. Fish, frogs, crayfish, turtle eggs, birds' eggs, small birds, mice, rabbits, squirrels, muskrats, domestic poultry--all are eagerly and rather impartially devoured.

The mink's menu consists of whatever he can catch as he wanders over his range. Naturally, his pursuit of the creatures which form his prey brings him into contact, and conflict, with man's interests. Since the mink does not choose his victims in accordance with man's ideas of ethics or economics, he alternates between the role of hero and that of villain, depending on what he happens to be feeding upon when observed. If he is cleaning out the rats from a farmer's granary, he is hero of the hour, but when with equal industry he cleans out the adjacent chicken coop, he changes abruptly to the number one villain spot.

The duck hunter throbs with indignation over a duck nest destroyed by a mink, but chuckles agreeably when the same mink destroys the eggs of the snapping turtle. The trapper's ire is roused at the discovery of muskrat carcasses half eaten by mink, but his annoyance is greatly soothed by finding a high-priced mink in his trap later.

A Non-Social Animal

So far as is known, mink are solitary creatures except during the mating season, and while the young are with the mother. Since these are strictly family groups, they are not real exceptions, and the mink can be considered a non-social animal. Even the most unsociable creatures, however, must maintain some sort of touch with others of their kind, and the mink has evolved a communication system of his own.

At intervals throughout the mink range will be found stones, logs, or clumps of earth upon which each passing mink drops some dung and, probably, urine. The dung carries with it some of the anal gland secretion, which gives it a highly personal odor, so that each mink calling at this "mail box" can tell who has been there

Mink

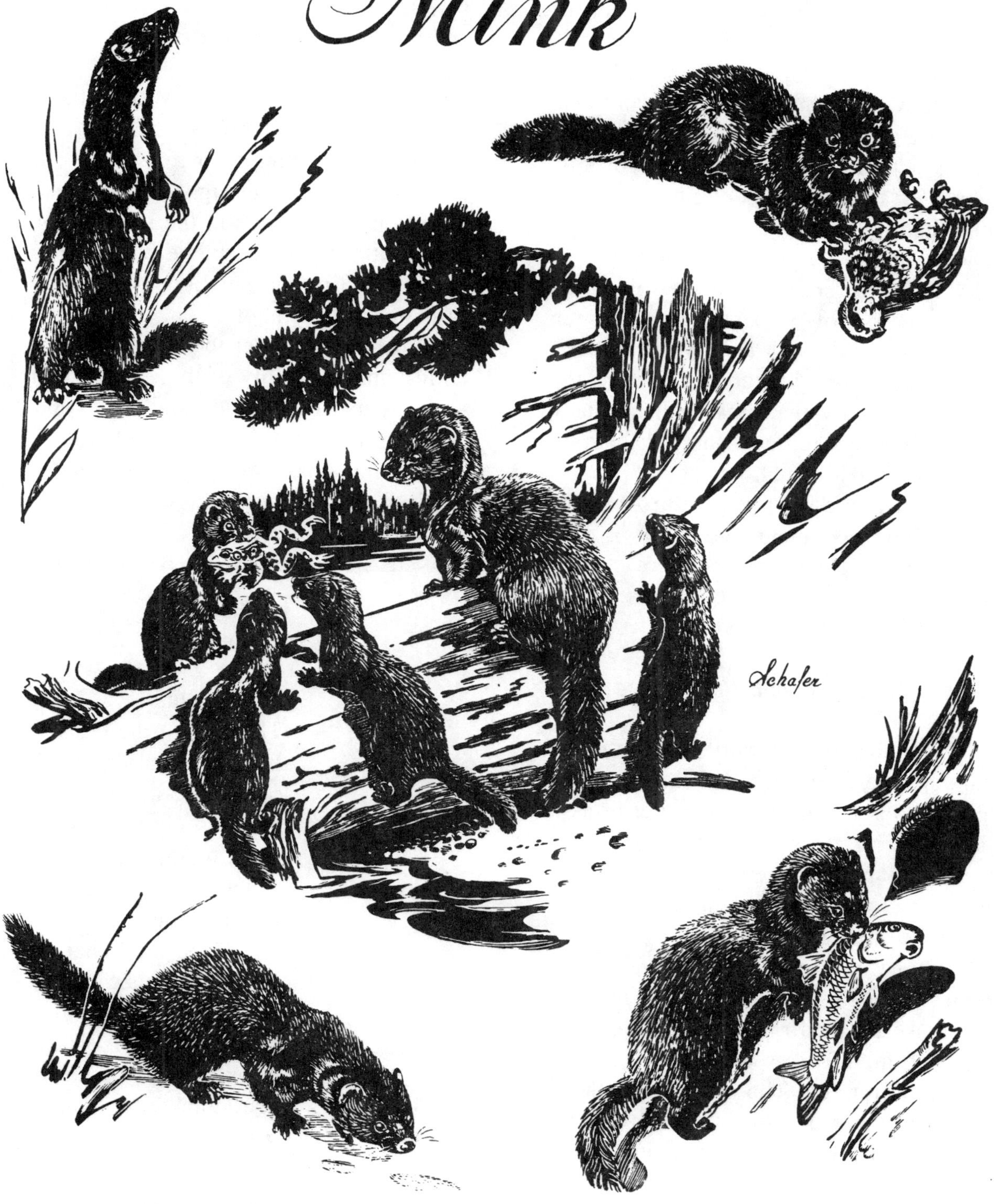

recently, and presumably the age, sex, and general condition of the late visitor. Such a crude communication system is familiar in the dog family, and the beaver also uses similar methods.

In the wilds, mink dens are usually near water, and may be in hollow logs, under stumps, or tree roots, or merely burrows in the bank. If the burrow is dug by the animal itself, it is about four inches in diameter, and of varying depth and length according to the character of the soil. In soft soil the burrow may be as much as ten or twelve feet in length and two or three feet in depth. Mink hunters, using specially trained dogs, track the mink to their dens or into temporary refuges, and kill them by various methods in such locations.

The young are born usually in April or May, and average about five or six per litter. In captivity, a wider range of numbers in litters is obtained than seems to be the rule under wild conditions.

Of Great Economic Importance

The mink is one of North America's most valuable fur bearers, whether considered as a domestic fur bearer or as a wild fur bearer. This is also true of the Great Lakes region where mink taken by trappers and hunters make up an important part of the annual fur crop.

Muskrats, raccoons, beavers, and mink are our major fur bearers. While many more muskrats than mink are taken every year, each mink pelt is worth much more than a muskrat pelt. The muskrat--"little brother" to the beaver--is still the champion fur producer in the region and North America, but the mink is providing more competition for top position. Mink trappers take between ten and twenty thousand pelts every year.

Mink are frequently taken in traps set for muskrats and vice versa, so that it is impractical to have a different trapping period for each. For this reason, the mink and muskrat trapping seasons run concurrently.

Since the end of World War II, the general trend of fur prices has been downward, although their renewed popularity resulted in higher prices for some long-haired furs in the mid 1960's. Apparently, the mink, be he wild or a ranch-raised pastel mutation, is still the fashion status symbol.

When we consider the remarkable ability and versatility of the mink, we are almost persuaded that the old adage about "Jack of all trades, but master of none," should in his case, be revised to read "Jack of all trades and master of all."

Mink
Mustela vison

Size:	1.3-3 pounds
Range:	Throughout the Great Lakes region and much of North America.
Habitat:	Wooded or swampy areas within sight of water.
Fact:	Because mink are at the top of the food chain they accumulate certain toxic chemicals from the environment. These chemicals may affect the animals' survival and reproduction.

The Otter--
Playboy of the Water

Probably no North American mammal is so well known yet so seldom seen as a wild otter. Everyone has seen pictures of otters. Most of us know that they catch fish and love to slide down hill, but how many have ever observed an otter in the wild?

So difficult is it to see otter that even many persons who live in the northern areas where otter are most abundant have never actually seen one, and an accurate estimate of the number of otter in any large area is almost impossible.

So difficult is it to see otter that even many persons who live in the northern areas where otter are most abundant have never actually seen one.

This lack of observational data is due partly to the secretive habits of the animal, and partly to its wandering proclivities.

While beavers are also aquatic mammals, and probably more nocturnal in their habits than otters, beavers live in colonies, with obvious evidence of their presence in the form of lodges, dams, canals, and timber cuttings. Hence, one knows where to find beavers and can observe them at dusk when they are about their daily chores.

Otters live in concealed holes along a river bank, construct no visible structures, and spend most of their lives traveling along the streams of a considerable region.

Otters are Restless Animals

An individual otter may range as much as 25 miles up and down a river and often makes overland trips to other rivers, lakes, and ponds. Always frequenting the water, or the near vicinity of water, the otter finds its ideal surroundings in good-sized clear streams that abound with fish, with a variety of pools, log jams, and overhanging banks. While the animals generally follow the streams in traveling, they like to take short cuts, and go overland to avoid horseshoe curves or hairpin turns. In addition, they frequently go overland from one stream or lake to another, even as far as 10 or 12 miles.

So restless are the creatures, they seldom stay more than a few days in one place, even though fish and other food may be extremely abundant. The Indians had a saying that "otter not happy in heaven."

An otter family is likely to have a route which it follows as regularly as a southern Methodist circuit rider. Sometimes it may be only 15 or 20 miles, often double that, and members of the family cover the route in from two to four weeks, passing through chains of ponds, up and down streams, and across lots between these water bodies.

This continual ranging makes it difficult to estimate otter populations, and to compare conditions in different parts of the region, or conditions in different years.

Early estimates of the otter population probably were low. One otter to eight square miles was once thought to be representative of the best otter habitat. However, in 1961, the results of the trapping season in one state revealed that in the best otter country there might be a somewhat higher population. Obviously, otter were never really abundant, in the sense that beaver were abundant, even in primitive times.

Fierce Fighters

Just why otter never became abundant, even under complete protection from man, is hard to understand, since they do not seem to have many natural enemies to contend with and their food supply is apparently entirely adequate for an increased number of otter. No known North American animal found in otter territory is capable of killing them in the water, and there is little evidence that many are killed on land.

A bear, wolf, a coyote, or a bobcat could undoubtedly kill even an adult otter if the latter were surprised some distance from water, but the otter is a fierce and dangerous fighter, and could hold his own against any lesser opponent. In England, where otter hunting with specially trained dogs is an ancient and honorable sport, an otter is considered as more than a match for all but a few exceptionally powerful dogs on land, and it is considered suicidal for any dog to tackle an otter in the water.

Otters are preeminently fish eaters.

Otters are preeminently fish eaters, although they vary their diet with crayfish, frogs, shellfish, etc. Anyone who has studied their food habits is struck with the abundance of crayfish and aquatic insect remains at their feeding places.

While trout anglers are inclined to view the otter as a dangerous competitor who lives on the biggest and best trout, the facts seem to be that otters catch such fish as are most readily available, and are likely to catch more of the rough, slow types such as suckers or carp, than of the speedy, elusive trout.

Investigations using otter stomachs obtained during the open trapping seasons, indicated that the otter is seldom a predator of determinative importance on either trout streams or other waters.

The fur of otter is one of the best, handsomest, and most durable on the market, and has been considered the standard of comparison for all others. Strangely enough it has not always been in great demand. However, in the 1950's, prices paid for otter pelts more than doubled while beaver prices dropped 70 percent. By the early 1960's, trappers were getting $25 for an otter and only $17 for a beaver pelt. Interest in otter trapping increased accordingly.

Must be Taught to Swim

Most observers agree that otters pair off, and that the mating season is toward the end of February. The gestation period seems to be about 60 days, and the young number from one to four.

The eyes are closed at birth, and the little animals appear almost black in color. Young otters are said to be reluctant to enter the water, and become accustomed to the watery element by riding into it on the mother's back. In fact, swimming and fish catching seem to be acquired by training or imitation, rather than by instinctive reactions. This is more or less characteristic of mammals with a high degree of intelligence, whose young must

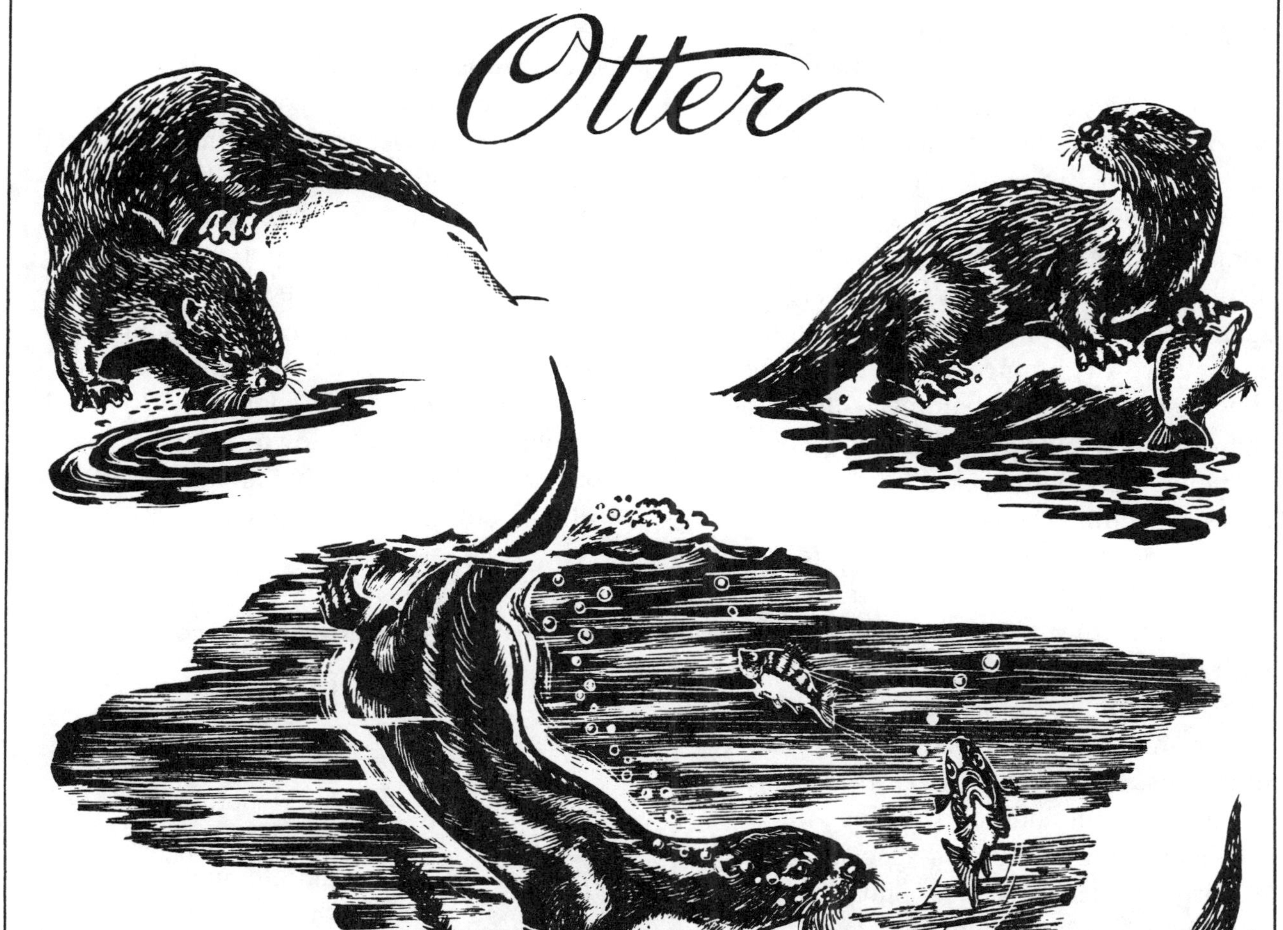
Otter
Schafer

be protected and trained for relatively long periods.

One of the characteristics most noticeable in the otter is his spirit of playfulness. Every observer who has seen otters in the wild or in captivity has commented on the genuine love of fun displayed by these animals. They are seldom still except when asleep, but are continually swimming, rolling, tumbling, chasing each other, or sliding with all the abandon of small boys with new sleds.

Otters play with each other, but they also play with various objects, such as sticks, stones, old cans, etc. They roll these objects on the ground, toss them into the water, dive after them, play tug of war with them, and generally enjoy them. Such a use of appliances for games is considered one of the highest attributes of the mammals, and perhaps finds its climax in the otter; for in addition to using appliances, the otter has a special performing place--the otter slide, or in human terms, the toboggan slide.

Play Instinct Highly Developed

Many hunters and naturalists have watched otters at their favorite amusement of coasting for as much as 30 or 40 feet down a steep slope, then climbing back up again and again just for the fun of sliding. Sometimes, a single otter does this; sometimes a family enjoys the sport together. One observer reported an otter making the climb and slide 22 times in rapid succession. This habit of sliding is not confined to ice or snow, but is carried on wherever otter are found, and may be done on grassy slopes or clay banks, wherever a smooth, steep, sliding spot can be located.

It is a normal occurrence for young mammals to play, and occasionally adults indulge in a sham fight or a chase for sport, but perhaps the otter is the only case where the entire race, young and old, unite to maintain a system of play not connected with the instincts of feeding, fighting, or multiplying, but simply for the sheer fun and exhilaration of the sport itself.

From a human viewpoint, it seems regrettable that otters are so difficult to observe, and so seldom seen, for think of the people who would congregate to watch an otter family slide down hill, and the business which could be done by a resort which could boast such a spectacle!

Otters
Lutra canadensis

Size:	11 to 31 pounds
Range:	Northern Great Lakes region although as far south in Michigan as Kalamazoo and throughout Wisconsin.
Habitat:	Streams and lakes, usually secluded and clear.
Fact:	Otter sometimes build homes in abandoned beaver lodges. Maximum life expectancy is about 13 years in the wild.

The Skunk--
Master of Defense

The skunk is a member of the *Mustelidae*, or weasel family, but like the otter, he is by no means a typical member of his family. The otter has become modified through ages of evolution into a streamlined aquatic playboy, an efficient inhabitant of streams and lakes. The skunk has become a slow, philosophical grubber for mice and insects, ill-equipped for any contest of speed or strength; yet, in a sense, master of all he surveys.

Unlike most members of the weasel family, the skunk does not tend to disappear as civilization advances. In most places the skunk is as numerous as he ever was, since his food resources are increased rather than diminished by rural settlement, while his natural enemies are reduced.

Litters Range From Four to Ten

Skunks live in burrows, and are perfectly capable of digging their own, but, like so many other mammals, they will take possession of a woodchuck hole when one is available. In winter, at least, skunks and woodchucks may be found in the same burrow, but at this time the woodchuck is neatly curled up in some barricaded corner fast asleep, and the skunks occupy the main part of the burrow.

Skunks may also move into caves, hollow stumps, or loose stone piles, and frequently seek lodging under a barn or house, to the consternation of the legal human owners or occupants. Summer cottages seem particularly attractive to skunks as residential possibilities, and even such nationally famous institutions as the Interlochen Music Camp have been temporarily upset by the unscheduled appearance of our little black and white friends on the orchestra platform.

An annual litter of from four to ten "kittens" is produced, usually between the middle of April and the middle of June, after a gestation period of about 63 days. Litters up to 16 have been reported, and perhaps a second litter is occasionally produced, but these are exceptional.

Scent Glands Can Be Removed

The young stick pretty close to the den for a time, but by midsummer are following the mother on her nightly forays. They are most attractive little fellows, so clean in their black and white coats and huge tails, and they frolic like domestic kittens.

Many a city child visiting the country has brought some "little woods kitties" back to the house after a stroll in the woods, since the little fellows are perfectly friendly and just "the cutest little things you ever saw." Actually they can make nice pets when young, and are just as easy to handle and as well behaved as real kittens. However, few households are willing to take a chance and the "woods kitties" are usually hustled carefully but firmly back into the woods from whence they came.

It is a simple operation to remove the

scent glands so that the skunks are entirely harmless, and such disarmed animals are frequently kept as pets. People with tendencies toward practical joking delight in watching the panic of unsuspecting visitors when their pet sunk walks into the room and jumps playfully onto the visitor's lap!

Prospective pet skunk owners should realize that older skunks are likely to get a bit crotchety and that skunks are among the many carriers of rabies. Although not protected by laws of many states, it is not legal in many states to possess live skunks taken from the wild. Normally, pet skunks are purchased from licensed skunk breeders. But given their tendency to bite once mature, these are not the best pets and people should be discouraged from keeping them.

Prospective pet skunk owners should realize that older skunks are likely to get a bit crotchety and that skunks are among the many carriers of rabies.

Insects are the staple food of the skunk, mainly beetles, grasshoppers, and the like. The number of insects eaten is enormous, and must aid the farmer and fruit grower considerably. Mice are also eaten in large numbers.

Yet in spite of his obvious value as an insect and mouse destroyer, some farmers seem aware only of the skunk's occasional raid on the poultry yard or apiary, and kill him whenever opportunity arises.

The fur of the skunk is deep, rich, glossy, and on a skin which makes strong and durable leather when dressed. In other words, it is an ideal fur. But it has been sadly discounted by the fierce and persistent smell which it is associated. Even though modern methods are able to cope successfully with this handicap, the fashion whims of milady have kept the skunk and other long-haired furs from gaining the high regard reserved for the mink.

Skunk Makes Excellent Eating

The skunk has always been eaten by Indians and by backwoods trappers. Its flesh is white, tender, and sweet, beautifully marked with fat and lean like the finest grade of pork.

Such is the unanimous testimony of all who have tasted the meat. It must, of course, be carefully prepared to avoid the taint from the scent glands, and it is unlikely that skunk steaks will ever be listed on the menus of famous restaurants, at lease under that name.

Although the skunk is a fur bearer, an efficient aid to the farmer in his incessant battle against insect and rodent pests, and an interesting, if unorthodox pet, it is not because of these things that the word "skunk" has assumed its notorious position in the English language. To call a man a "skunk" is about as insulting as anything which could be said, and implies very grave defects in the moral character of the individual so mentioned. This is most unfair to the animal from whom the name is taken, for the skunk is really one of the gentlest, most inoffensive creatures in the world. Let the skunk alone, and he will let you alone.

If, however, the enemy follows and overtakes him, as a man may do, he turns and faces about, as if to say, "OK, if you must have it, come ahead," But even then he gives further warning by stamping his feet, and raising the big tail, all but the white tip, which still hangs downward.

SKUNK

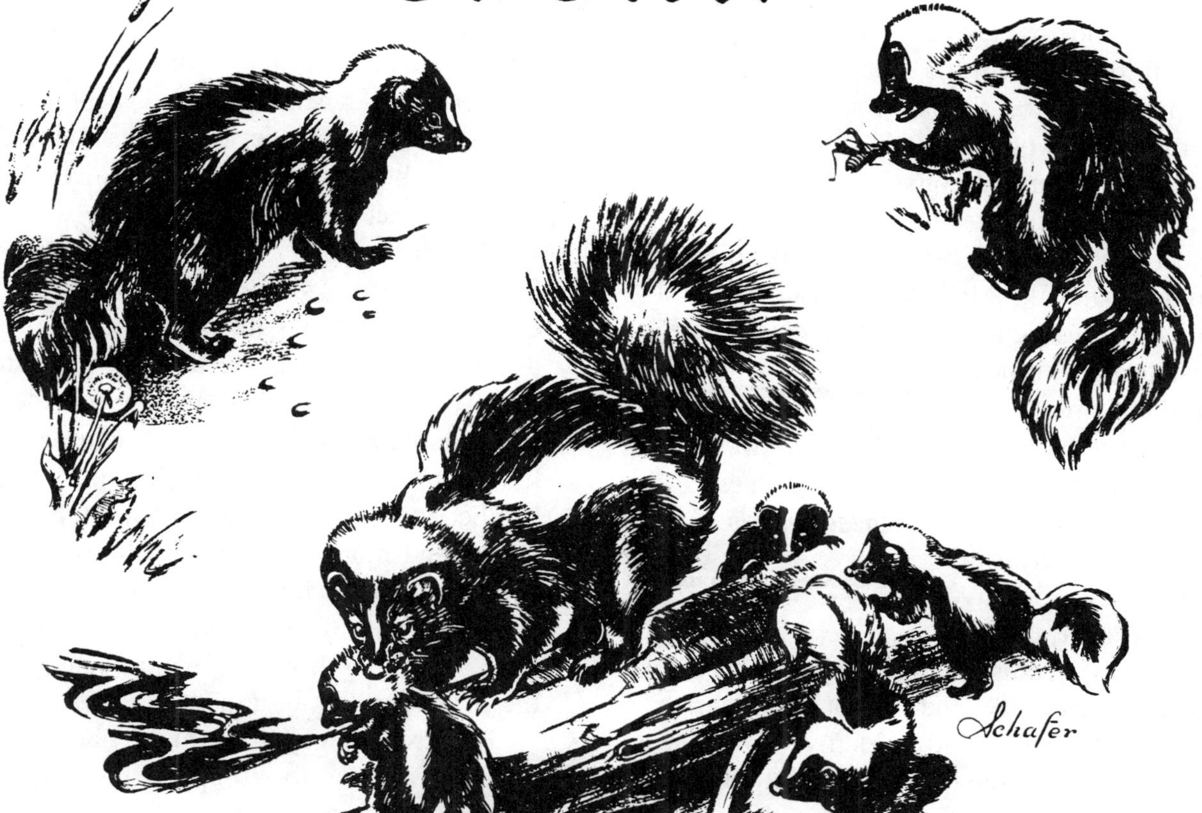

Now beware, for if the tip comes up too it means not "surrender," but "clear for action." One more step means "bombs away," and few creatures are still in condition to finish the attack after that happens, for the skunk's smell gun is justly famous the world around.

This armament consists of two large glands under the tail, which secrete and eject a liquid fluid like musk, but infinitely more powerful. All of the weasel family possess these glands, but they reach their spectacular climax in the skunk.

All of the weasel family possess these glands.

The glands are situated on each side of the anus; the two ducts from them are ordinarily hidden away within the rectum, but can be protruded for quick service, like the gun of a submarine. The fluid is clear and golden-yellow in color, with an intensely acid reaction, and appears faintly luminous in the dark, like phosphorescent light. Many attempts have been made to describe the odor of fresh skunk fluid to someone who has never experienced it, but such attempts are largely futile.

"Almost Impregnable" Defense

If this powerful spray actually strikes the intruder, it causes temporary blindness, coughing, and choking, nausea, and even fainting. At some distance, or after a lapse of time, it becomes merely a strongly disagreeable odor.

The distance to which the spray can be thrown is somewhere between six and ten feet; further, of course, with aid from the wind. The number of times the gun can be fired and the amount of fluid given off vary from the size of the skunk and the time elapsed since its last use. Ordinarily, each gland contains enough for five or six rounds and, if entirely emptied, would require about a week for a complete refill.

The skunk is an interesting example of what happens when an individual, a species, or a nation develops an apparently "impregnable" defense system and rests its future on that system.

We all remember what happened to France, with its "impregnable" Maginot Line. The skunk has likewise undergone a degenerative process. He has lost the slim form, the amazing speed and agility, the indomitable ferocity, and sheer courage of his cousins, the weasel and the mink, and has become a slow, lazy amiable bug hunter and mouse digger, unable to conquer his prey by speed or power, and an easy victim for such enemies as the great horned owl, which is unaffected by the disgusting spray gun.

He has exchanged the many native talents of his family group for just one, and "almost impregnable" defense.

Skunk

Mephitis mephitis

Size:	3.3 to 11 pounds (larger in captivity)
Range:	Throughout the Great Lakes region.
Habitat:	A mix of forests and fields although does well in a suburban environment.
Fact:	Most "pet" skunks are destroyed when mature because of their tendency to bite.

The Badger--
Living Steam Shovel

The badger, like the mink, otter, and skunk, is a member of the *Mustelidae*, or weasel family. But like the skunk, it has become somewhat of a specialist and has lost many of the typical weasel characteristics.

Whereas the skunk has lost speed, strength and cunning as well as the slim form of the typical weasel, the badger has lost only speed and slimness. Strength and cunning the badger possesses in plenty, but his form has become squat, compact, and massive.

He is about two feet long, extraordinarily low hung and broad, and when curled up asleep, with hairs erect, looks like a well-stuffed cushion. On the other hand, when lying or crawling on the ground, he is so flat and broad as to suggest a huge, hairy turtle.

The legs are short and thick, and the large feet are provided with long and very strong claws, making them powerful digging tools. The head is broad and massive, with round furry ears and jaws filled with formidable teeth.

The loose hair or "fur" is a grizzled mixture of black, white, gray or tawny, each hair having most of these colors on some part of its length, and the whole blending into rather a handsome coat.

Has Indomitable Spirit

The whole appearance of the badger is one of great muscular power, and this power is controlled by a capable brain and an indomitable spirit. The badger's strength and spirit made him the object of a unique form of sport in the British Isles--badger baiting. To this sport (?) our language owes its expressive verb "to badger," that is, to harass or annoy.

The badger's strength and spirit made him the object of a unique form of sport.

In this contest, the badger was placed in a barrel, or half barrel, laid on its side on the ground, and dogs were set upon him. Since only a few dogs at a time could get at the badger, he was often able to do considerable damage before being dragged into the open. Dogs were judged according to their ability to haul the animal out of its shallow hole, and were specially trained for this performance.

The American badger is similar to the European badger, although a little smaller. Badgers were abundant in prairie areas when this country was first explored and settled, and Wisconsin was called the "Badger State." Since the activities of badgers sometimes interfere with farming practices, the animals are no longer abundant, although by no means rare, in their former range.

Still Found In The Region

Edwin Lincoln Moseley, writing a number of years ago about "Our Wild

Animals," declared that "Badgers have never been found much farther east than Indiana and were probably never very common in that state. Their range includes much of the country farther west and extends into Canada and Mexico." He added, "At least one popular encyclopedia and one well-written book of natural history state that they have disappeared from Michigan, Ohio, Indiana, Illinois, Wisconsin, Minnesota, and Iowa.

This is a mistake, they still live in many places in Michigan and Wisconsin and in some localities, probably, in every one of the states mentioned.

Moseley refers to tales he had heard, years ago, about the "mysterious animal that digs into graves at night." The badger's preference for cemeteries he explains as "probably due merely to the fact that it prefers high and dry places for its burrows, and in some flat regions, which were formerly not well drained, the people selected for burying grounds the gravel or sand ridges and knolls."

The badger feeds upon whatever animal food he can catch and kill, principally the ground squirrels, gophers, and field mice among which he lives. It is beyond his ability to chase and capture these nimble creatures, for the badger is slow and clumsy; but it is easy for him to dig them out of their ground burrows and dens, as the badger is one of the world's best diggers.

The badger feeds upon whatever animal food he can catch and kill, principally the ground squirrels, gophers, and field mice among which he lives.

When a badger starts to dig he just seems to disappear into the earth in a shower of dirt, and woe to the gopher or mouse at the other end of the burrow. While his destruction of gophers and mice may be meritorious, the excavations which he makes in their pursuit excite the wrath of the farmer, and may lead to the eventual elimination of the badger.

Interestingly, badgers are now appearing in close proximity to rural developments. Woodlots thought to contain little in the way of wildlife may host a badger family.

Badger Never Surrenders

The entrance to the badger's own burrow is large, and the tunnel reaches below the frost line. The animal changes its abode frequently, and digs more holes than it needs, thereby saving considerable labor for coyotes, foxes, rabbits, snakes, etc., which take advantage of its abandoned excavations.

The young are born in May or June and usually number from two to five per litter. The family is believed to remain together until midsummer or later, when they probably scatter to establish homes of their own. Little is known about the details of family life, since it is spent largely underground.

As already indicated, the badger has sacrificed speed, agility and grace for strength and digging power. This strength serves him well for defense, and he is not al all averse to a fight. "Come one, come all" might well be the badger's slogan, for he fears no odds and never surrenders. Few dogs are able to hold their own with an adult badger, and coyotes seldom, if ever, attack a badger singlehanded. The badger fights with a savage snarling ferocity which daunts most opponents and leaves him in possession of the arena.

Despite this strength and belligerence,

BADGER

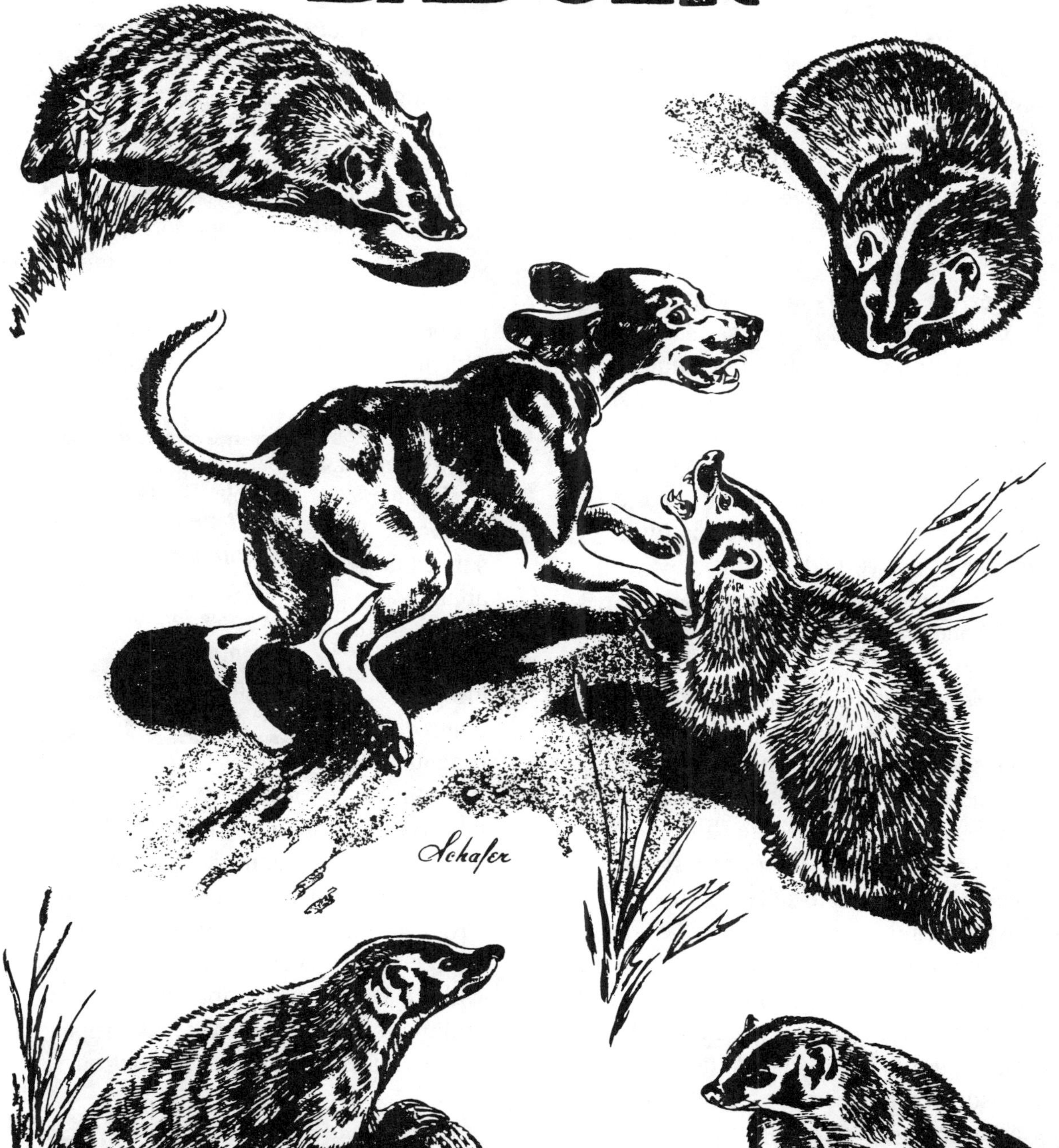

young badgers make lovable pets, and are comical as well as affectionate. Tame badgers love to romp and play with other animals as well as with human associates. Many who have seen movies of badgers have chuckled over the antics of the young badger.

Badgers are known to have romped and tussled with foxes, puppies, kittens, and other animals in captivity. Apparently a young badger will play with most any other creature which is at hand and shows a reciprocal spirit. As he grows older, however, his play is likely to become too rough-house for less robust companions. His playful nips draw blood, and his friendly blows tear skin or clothing like paper. An adult badger does not make a trustworthy playmate. If left to his own devices, the captive badger will play with balls, sticks, feeding dishes, or whatever may be handy.

May Leave Retreats in Winter

Being nocturnal in habit, and spending the day underground, badgers are seldom observed by people. They are, however, abroad during daylight hours occasionally, and when discovered usually attempt to hide by flattening themselves on the ground like a slight hummock in a field. So flat do they lie, and so grasslike does their coat appear, that they often escape detection even from a short distance.

If disturbed in this pose, the animal may assume an air of belligerence and charge the intruder. This is mostly bluff, intended to disconcert the opponent, and the badger scuttles off looking for an escape burrow.

During the coldest weather, especially while the ground is frozen, badgers hibernate in their burrows, yet badgers have been observed outside their retreats during every month in the year as far north as Minnesota and Michigan.

Safety in Small Numbers

Badger fur is thick and coarse, and is not in much demand by furriers. Badgers are not of much importance as fur bearers in the region since only one to two hundred per year are reported taken by trappers. Since the badger is so industrious and energetic in his search for mice, gophers, ground squirrels and other small rodents, he probably is of considerable value as a rodent control agent.

Badgers are not sufficiently abundant, however, to be a very effective control on rodents.

Badgers are not sufficiently abundant, however, to be a very effective control on rodents, and the annoyance caused by their digging proclivities probably offsets the beneficial results of their rodent destruction.

In the Great Lakes region there is no strong pro-badger or anti-badger sentiment, and perhaps it may be allowed to exist without benefit of campaigns for its elimination as a menace or its propagation as a species in danger of extinction.

Badger
Taxidea taxus

Size:	13-24 pounds
Range:	Throughout the Great Lakes states. Rare in Ontario.
Habitat:	Prefers mix of woodlands and open country. The badger primarily lives and hunts in the open fields secluded from human activity.
Fact:	It appears as though badgers are adapting well to human occupation and are found in farming areas as well as some rural areas.

The Wolverine, Marten, Fisher...
King-Size Weasels

The fisher, marten, and wolverine are included in this series because even though the first two are found in the region by reintroduction and the wolverine is no longer found here, they are interesting members of the weasel family. Also, the fisher and marten were once important fur bearers in the Great Lakes region.

The Wolverine

The wolverine is the giant of the weasel family, and the animal from which Michigan derives its nickname, the "Wolverine State." Just why Michigan acquired this name is obscure, since the wolverine was certainly never common in the state. In fact, it has never been proved that any wolverine ever lived in Michigan other than as a denizen of some zoo.

The best we can do is to conjecture that, since wolverine did live in Canada and in the northern Minnesota area, they may have lived in northern Michigan also. It is also odd that an animal of so notorious a reputation was chosen to represent the state. If we judge the wolverine for his reputation among people who live in the areas which he inhabits we must admit that he is far from a model to be emulated.

The wolverine is also known in literature as the carajou, karkajou, glutton, and skunkbear. A big wolverine is about four feet in length, tail included, and weighs about 25 pounds. The animals are deep brown in color, with bands of chestnut along the sides, and irregular spots or patches of yellowish white. There is a great variation in color, and size and distribution of spots and bands.

The wolverine is found in Alaska and northern and western Canada and also has made a comeback in some northwestern states, now being found in numbers in states such as Washington, Oregon, Idaho, and Montana.

Powerful, intelligent, and with a taste for every sort and condition of flesh, the wolverine has little trouble in finding summer food. Woodchucks, ground squirrels, fish, grogs, hares, rats, mice, birds, eggs, and any bit of carrion available are eaten eagerly. If meat is hard to get the wolverine ekes out his menu with berries.

In winter, his fare is tremendously reduced. Most of his summer prey has migrated southward or is hibernating beyond his reach in the frozen earth underneath the snow. Snowshoe hares, ptarmigan, and pickings from deer or caribou killed by wolves are about all he can get.

Thus it is that the wolverine follows the trap line, stealing the trapped animals, before the trapper can reach them, while cunningly evading the unsprung traps; locates the food cache near the trapper's cabin and tears it apart and breaks into the cabin itself to create havoc.

The Marten

The marten, or pine marten as it is usually called, occurred originally throughout the coniferous forests in North America, from the Central States to the Arctic Ocean. It was so plentiful that it periodically overflowed certain areas and spread in all directions, appearing in territory where it was previously rare or unknown.

On the other hand, periods of scarcity seem to have occurred, indicating that martens were subject to cycles like the snowshoe hare and many other wild animals.

Martens are beautiful creatures, rich dark yellowish brown in color, shading into blackish on the tail and legs, with whitish ear linings, and with a large irregular patch of pale buff or orange on the throat and breast.

The winter fur is thick, soft, an inch or more in depth, of the richest hue, and has scattered through it coarse black hairs which the furrier pulls out. The tail is bushy, and when seen in trees the marten gives the impression of a large dark squirrel, with white ears and a yellow throat; when on the ground, he looks like a dark-colored young fox.

The body is long and supple, the legs short, and the toes separate, with long sharp claws. The average weight is about four pounds. Martens exhibit great agility and grace of movement, spending most of their lives in trees, where they den in hollows like squirrels or raccoons. The young are brought forth in litters of six to eight early in the spring.

Martens thrive in wilderness areas, and with the disappearance of the great coniferous forests in the region, the marten disappeared also. By the early 1930's it was apparent that they were gone from the bulk of the Great Lakes region.

Martens often take to trees, and prefer the denser part of the forests, but they often descend to the ground for food, especially in winter when they hunt for hares, grouse, and other ground-living species, which they trail by scent as well as by sight. Their broad feet enable them to move easily and quickly even on soft snow.

Martens have little to fear from native enemies; their big cousin the fisher is said to kill them at times, and the great horned owl may take one on occasion, but few carnivores care to taste their flesh unless driven by extreme hunger.

Martens have little to fear from native enemies.

Man is chief enemy of the marten, and exercises his menace in two ways: first by cutting down the dense forests which are the natural habitat of the animals; and secondly, by trapping them for their beautiful fur. Martens are intensely curious, and among the easiest of all fur bearers to catch in traps.

Although early projects failed, subsequent attempts to reintroduce the marten appear to have been successful in parts of Michigan's Upper Peninsula.

The Fisher

The fisher, also called pekan, is remarkable for its size--length about two feet, plus another foot of tail, and for its dog-like head.

The average weight of a fisher is eight

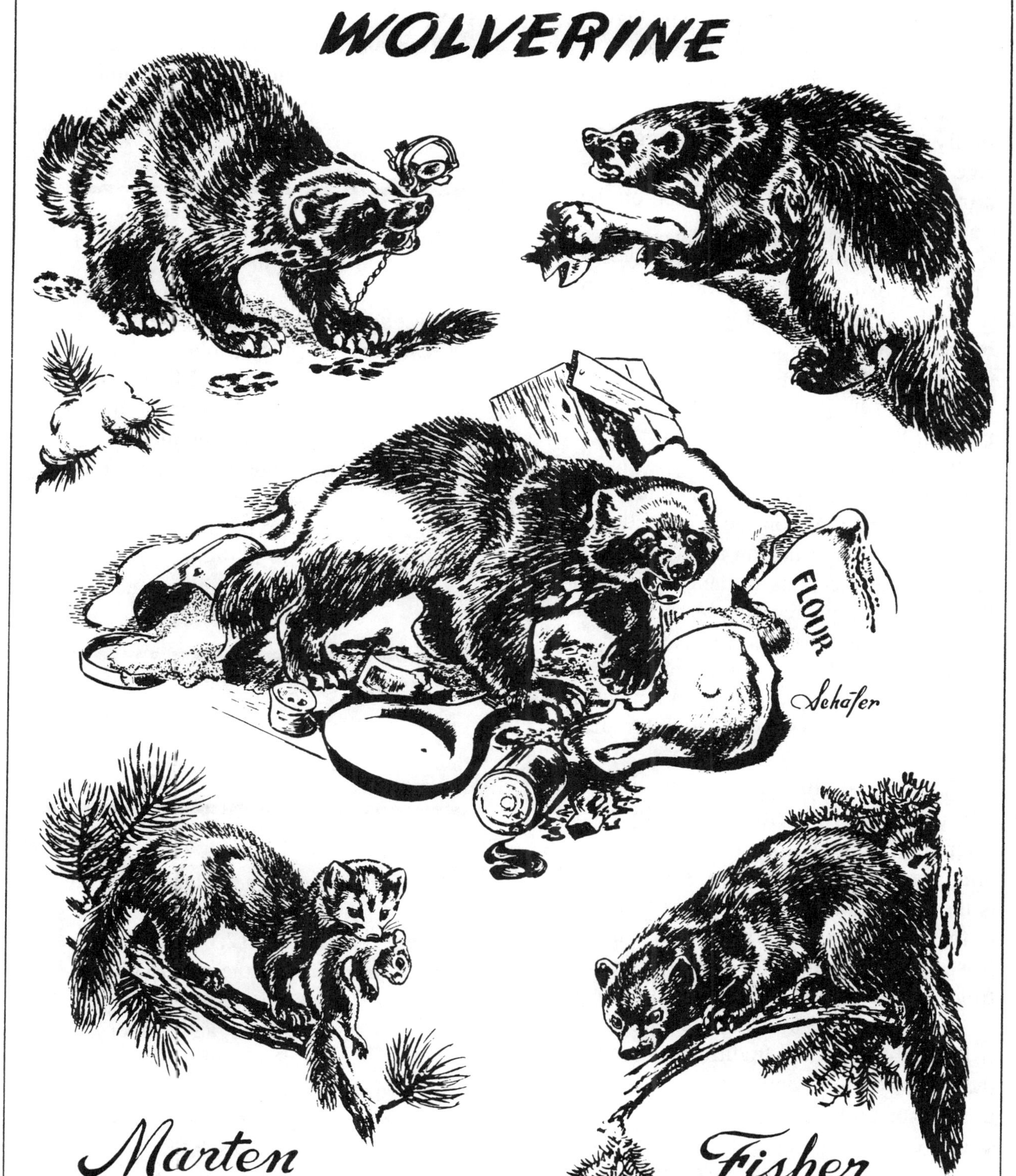
WOLVERINE
FLOUR
Schafer
Marten
Fisher

to ten pounds, although specimens have been taken which weighed up to 18 pounds. Fishers are grayish brown to brownish black in color, much more solidly built than martens, and suggest a huge black cat with a bushy tail when seen in trees, or a black fox when seen on the ground.

Since this animal is not primarily a catcher of fish, much question has arisen as to why it received the name "fisher." Probably the name was given to distinguish it from its smaller cousin. The "pine" marten lives in the pine woods of the uplands, the "fisher" marten in the lowlands and swamps.

In general habits the fisher is just a big marten, living more on the ground than in the trees, although he can and does catch squirrels and raccoons in their leafy haunts. The fisher is capable of remarkable speed for a short run or short climb, and can catch most any kind of small mammal in this initial sprint. The fisher is one of the few creatures known to successfully attack the porcupine.

Porcupine quills seem to have little effect on the fisher, either internally or externally, although other mammals are often fatally injured by the quills. So fierce is the fisher that it is said to kill bear cubs in the den while the mother bear is away. It is a good swimmer, and catches fish, frogs, and other aquatic animals in season.

When attacked by men or dogs, the fisher fights with the traditional ferocity of the weasel family, and gives a good account of himself against any odds. The young usually two or three, are born in a hollow tree or log in early spring.

Fishers formerly were found over most of the Great Lakes states retreating before the axe and trap until they probably disappeared entirely, although there was the possibility a few stragglers might have survived.

Reintroduction attempts date back to the 1950's and in recent years fisher numbers have been on the increase.

Marten

Martes americana

Size: 1.6-3.3 pounds

Range: Ontario and much of northern Michigan.

Habitat: Upland forests of spruce, hemlock, fir, and sometimes white cedar.

Fact: Lives about 13 years in the wild. Clear cutting is a threat to survival.

Fisher

Martes pennanti

Size: 4.4-12.1 pound

Range: Northern Wisconsin, Minnesota, Michigan's Upper Peninsula, and Ontario.

Habitat: Dense coniferous woods.

Fact: Eats all but skin of

Wolf and Coyote--
Wild Dogs of Forests and Plains

It is not a flight of fancy to speak of wolves and coyotes as wild dogs, since they are, in truth, just that.

All of our domestic breeds of dogs not only belong to the same family, *Canidae*, but also to the same genus, *Canis*, as do the wolf and the coyote. Only in the species name do domestic dogs and wild dogs differ in scientific classification.

There might even be some question about the species differentiation, since dogs, wolves, and coyotes are able to breed together, and the hybrids so produced are also fertile. In fact, the famous husky dog of Alaska is a hybrid, part wolf, part dog.

The wolf is one of the best-advertised creatures in existence, having been the subject of folk lore, hunting legend, and outdoor story from time immemorial. Some of his alleged characteristics are even translated, or perhaps parodied, in slang to designate humans. As, for example, we speak of a "wolf" of Wall Street, or more familiarly, a "wolf" in affairs with the opposite sex. Both of these types are unfair to "canine union number one," the true wolves.

Wolf Has Several Aliases

The wolves of North America, while differing in size and color in various parts of the continent, are on the whole very similar in characteristics, and are much more nearly alike than are the many varieties of domestic dogs. Like so many other notorious characters, the wolf is known under several aliases. Among them are gray wolf, timber wolf, buffalo wolf, lobo, big wolf, and northern wolf.

In general, with the exception of the huge wolves of Alaska, wolves run about three and a half feet in length, excluding the somewhat bushy tails, and weigh up to 100 pounds. An adult wolf is, of course, a formidable creature, and very few dogs stand a chance against a wolf in open combat.

Wolves do not breed until they are two or three years old. In the Great Lakes region, they mate for the season and possibly longer, in late January or February. The gestation period is about nine weeks. The den may be any suitable shelter, such as a cave, hollow log, or ground den. Three to a dozen whelps may be born, but usually only two or three survive to maturity.

In spring and summer small prey is abundant, and the wolves, wandering about by day and night, easily pick up a good living, and grow fat, lazy and good natured.

In spring and summer small prey is abundant, and the wolves, wandering about by day and night, easily pick up a good living.

As summer closes, and the whelps grow, the parents take them on hunting excursions, and show them what is good to eat and how to hunt for it. With the onset of winter, hard times set in also; the small creatures disappear, and wolves must call upon their strength and intelligence to outwit and overcome the larger animals upon which they now prey.

The peaceable disposition of summer changes as snow fills the forests, cold gales moan through the trees, and long cold nights enshroud an almost dead world. Then hungry ferocity, crafty patience, and daring make the wolf a formidable foe to everything which roams the forests. It is at this season that wolves travel in "packs," and assist each other in capturing prey.

The endurance of the wolf is amazing, yet most deer, antelope, and horses can out-speed and out-swim them, and would usually escape from a single wolf. Therefore, two or sometimes several unite, and by relieving one another, cutting across, and heading off the prey, more than make up for their lack of individual speed.

Whether or not wolves are dangerous to man has been debated for centuries. Much exaggeration has crept into the popular history of wolves, from the superstitious tales of old to the stirring stories of modern adventurers. While it must be considered doubtful that wolves will attack man today, even in the wildest parts of this continent, it is likely that they did so in more primitive times. The wolf is an intelligent animal, and modern man is the most dangerous creature on earth.

Wolves have come to know that man is the "untouchable," whose very presence is a peril, and experiences of various people in northern Canada indicate that wolves will not attack a lone man even under apparently extreme provocation. But early man, armed with clubs, spears, or bows, was quite a different proposition, and many tales of wolves attacking and killing lone persons, or even small groups, in northern Canada or Siberia seem well authenticated. Nevertheless, far more people have been scared than have been hurt; and that mainly by the terrific howling which multiplies itself in echoing volume, until it sounds as if the woods were full of wolves.

Wolves Increasing Their Range

In recent years there has been increasing public awareness of the value of wolves. In many respects, a wolf pack represents what is truly wild in the Great Lakes region. For this reason, and others, people have led the fight to end eradication of the wolf and, instead, protect it from harm.

Once nearly extinct from Michigan (except Isle Royale National Park in Lake Superior), the wolf has successfully expanded its range from west to east and is now found in packs in every county in Michigan's Upper Peninsula. Healthy populations continue to be found in northern Minnesota and Wisconsin as well as Ontario, Canada.

People can educate themselves enough about ecology to understand the important role wolves play in the natural world.

Tourists and residents alike thrill to spot a wolf, singly or in a pack, while traveling a highway where they are sometimes struck by cars and killed.

Perhaps the most important lesson to be learned from the wolf experience in the region is the

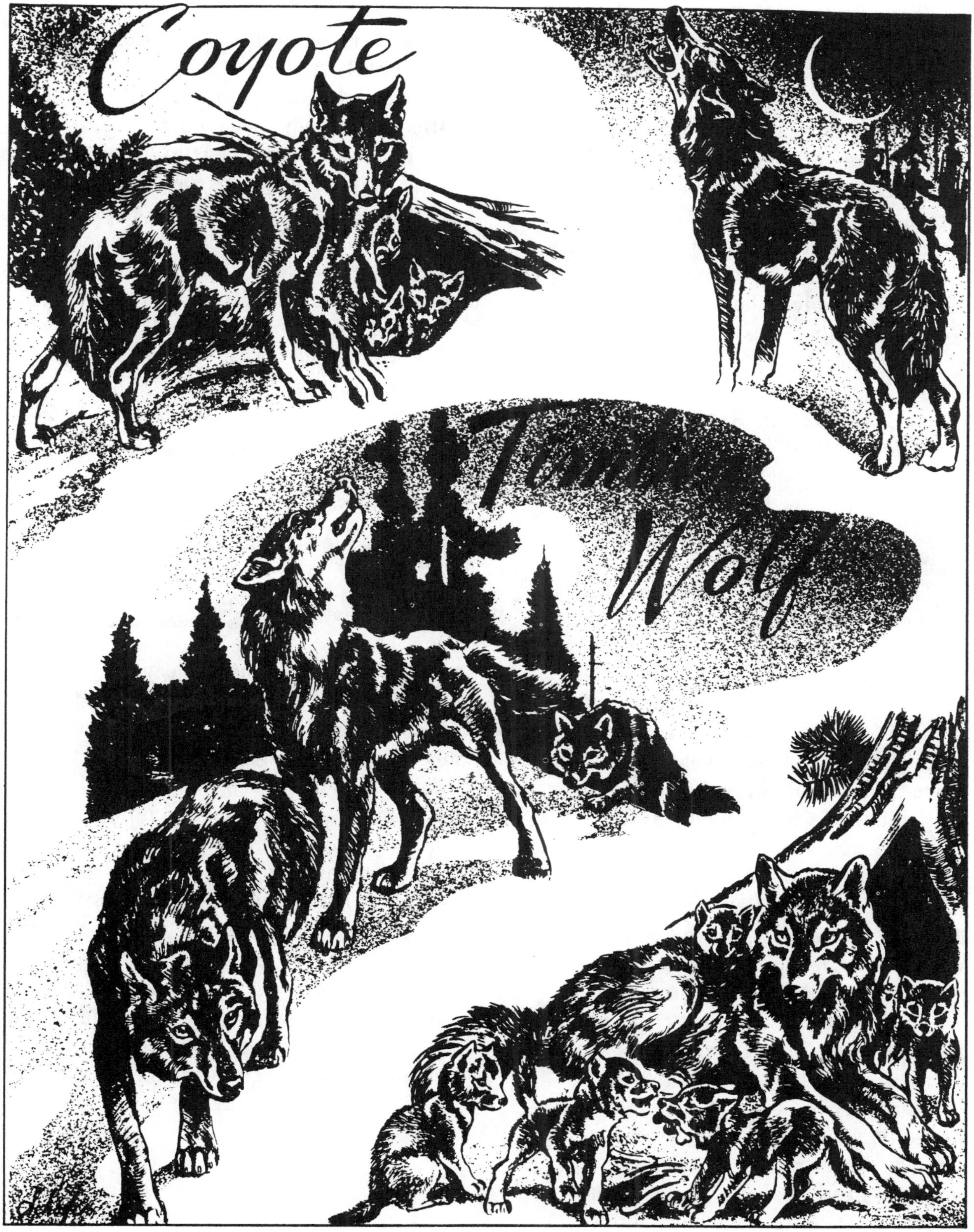
Coyote
Wolf

fact that people can educate themselves enough about ecology to understand the important role wolves play in the natural world. Worried deer hunters' fears about the effect of wolf populations on deer herds have been soothed as deer populations increase as wolf populations increase and spread throughout the region.

When traveling in the north country keep an ear ready to hear the lonely wolf howl in the night. It is a sign you are in the wilderness.

Coyote Expands Range, Numbers

Although the big timber wolf was once in danger of extinction in the Great Lakes region, the same cannot be said of the smaller cousin, the coyote.

The coyote is considerably smaller than the wolf, and can also be readily distinguished from the latter by the way in which he carries his tail. When running, the coyote carries his tail well down, not high up as does the wolf. There is much color variation among coyotes, from nearly white to nearly black, with varying proportions of yellowish and tawny.

The coyote is less majestic and imposing than the wolf, but much better adapted to life in the modern, so-called civilized, world. The wolf retreats before man, and his habitat is continually shrinking. The coyote welcomes man with his agriculture and attendant changes, and has expanded his range and his numbers in recent years.

Brushy cover, cutover lands, abandoned agricultural areas, are happy hunting grounds for the coyote. He is just a wild dog, and likes most everything to eat that a dog does. Mice, rats, ground squirrels, and birds are his natural foods. But these are eagerly supplemented by poultry and young livestock when man so generously breeds them and turns them out to roam in coyote territory.

Livestock corralled or stabled at night suffers little from coyote depredations, but it is not always practicable to handle stock in this way. Poultry, however, can be kept out of reach of coyotes and foxes if properly cared for. Much of the damage laid to the coyote is done by dogs, but certainly the animal cannot be whitewashed. He is not suitable company for poultry, sheep or calves, and should be controlled in agricultural areas. In areas where stock is not a major interest, or where stock can be protected, the coyote probably does more good as a rodent controller and scavenger than he does harm to game.

He is not suitable company for poultry, sheep or calves.

It is scarcely necessary to worry about his extermination, for he is too clever and adaptable to be in danger. We should not fall into the error so often seen in print, that the coyote is a miserable, cowardly rascal, worthy only of contempt.

He is a rather handsome, courageous, and clever creature, who is far too smart to fight against hopeless odds. How many men would pit a valued dog against a coyote of equal weight and how many men would care to step into an enclosure unarmed to try conclusions with an adult coyote, regardless of weight?

Wolf
Canis lupus

Size: 77-143 pounds

Range: Northern Minnesota, Wisconsin, Michigan's Upper Peninsula, and Ontario.

Habitat: The wolf prefers a mix of woodlands, swamps, and open areas where a variety of both small and large game can be found. Large areas undisturbed by man are preferred.

Fact: Wolves eat 4-13 pounds of meat per day, primarily in the form of small game and rodents.

Coyote
Canis latrans

Size: 24-46 pounds

Range: The coyote is found not only throughout the Great Lakes region but also throughout much of North America.

Habitat: A mix of wooded and open areas. More and more it is moving closer to developed areas.

Fact: Most coyotes live only 6 to 8 years in the wild.

The Red Fox--
Wise Guy of the Wild

The red fox is the traditional symbol of craft, cunning--and cleverness, and like most "wise guys," has contrived to make a lot of enemies. Even those who admire the fox for his cleverness do so in a grudging sort of way, and really esteem him more as an adversary worthy of the chase than as a character worthy of respect.

Over the years, no other animal has been subject to such bitter controversy and acrimonious debate as has the red fox. Let us ignore, for the moment, the question of whether the fox does more good by his rodent catching propensities than he does harm by his poultry and game catching tendencies, and consider him as an interesting inhabitant of our woods and fields.

Fox is Highly Adaptable

The fox is, of course, closely related to the dog, wolf, and jackal, belonging to the same great family, the *Canidae*, but to a different genus. Wolves, coyotes, dogs, and jackals belong to the genus *Canis*, while foxes belong to the genus *Vulpes*.

Foxes are smaller, more agile and delicate than are wolves and jackals, with a broader skull and sharper muzzle, larger ears, a longer, more bushy tail, and usually with longer fur. Weaker than his wolfish relatives, but endowed with great swiftness, and accustomed to playing the dual role of hunter and hunted, his brain has developed to a high degree to compensate for his bodily deficiencies, and shows capacity for still further development.

As has been pointed out by various naturalists, the sagacity of the fox is a little more proverbial than actual, and certainly is more apparent in populous regions than in the wilderness. This very fact, however, is a tribute to the intelligence of the fox, for it indicates a quality of mind above mere native half-instinctive knowledge. Since foxes display notable quickness in meeting new problems presented by changes in agricultural practices and the emergence of man, with his traps, guns, and poisons, the fox has been elevated to the rank of chief enemy--a comparatively novel state of things.

It is, in truth, this ability of the fox to survive and thrive amid the complexities of modern civilization that brings him into the limelight as a competitor of man, and which has made him the object of so much abuse and denunciation.

The fox has been elevated to the rank of chief enemy--a comparatively novel state of things.

Wide Variations in Size, Color

The red fox inhabits practically the whole northern hemisphere, and varies greatly in size and color in portions of his range. Our American form seems especially variable, since its typical yellowish-red color, darkest on the back and shoulders, may be very bright or very pale. Or it may have the markings on spine and withers very dark and distinct, making it a "cross fox;" or be totally black with white-tipped tail. Or the fox may be primarily black with the tips of most of the hairs white, giving the fur a frosted or silver appearance.

Such variations occur occasionally in wild stock, but have been perpetuated by selective breeding in domestic strains, and are now standard types in ranch foxes. All of these fancy types, however, are merely natural variations of the ordinary red fox.

Foxes everywhere are naturally burrowers and nocturnal hunters of ground-nesting birds from ducks and geese to sparrows, and of their eggs; rodents of every sort, frogs, lizards, snakes and insects; and also of various fruits and berries. Grass is often found in fox stomachs, but this is probably eaten in a casual way, just as a dog may frequently be observed biting off and swallowing grass and other herbage.

Foxes everywhere are naturally burrowers and nocturnal hunters of ground- nesting birds.

Some of the prey is taken by running it down, some by stalking it with crafty caution, some by lying motionless until the victim approaches close enough to be seized by a catlike pounce. The fare and the method vary from place to place, and endless stratagems match the native precautions of the quarry. All the larger carnivores are enemies of the fox under wilderness conditions, and the skill learned from generations of avoiding these carnivores serves the present-day fox well in evading the packs of hounds which man sets upon his trail.

Abundance Varies Tremendously

The gestation period of the fox is about 51 days, and the young are born in March or April, under natural conditions. The fox pups are blind during the first few days of their existence, and usually do not venture out of the den until they are three or four weeks old.

The home life of the fox is ideal, and both parents seem to share in the care and feeding of the offspring. Many observations have been made to prove the devotion of the mother fox to her young, and the courage with which she sometimes defends them. Mother foxes have even been known to attack large dogs when the safety of the fox puppies seemed threatened.

Although the fox is a native to most of the northern hemisphere, his abundance has always varied tremendously in different parts of his range. The fox is not a lover of either deep forest or vast prairies. He is rather a creature of the broken country, and always increases with pioneer agriculture.

In the Great Lakes region, foxes were apparently scarce when the white man first explored the state, increased greatly as the land was cleared and placed under cultivation, decreased with the development of intensive agriculture, and again increased during recent years.

The explanation for the recent increase is not clear, but is probably connected with shifts in agricultural practices.

The red fox, swift, cunning, and adaptable, finds more places to den in safety, more cover for concealment in escaping enemies and stalking prey, and more food in the form of small birds and mammals. In other words, the situation is

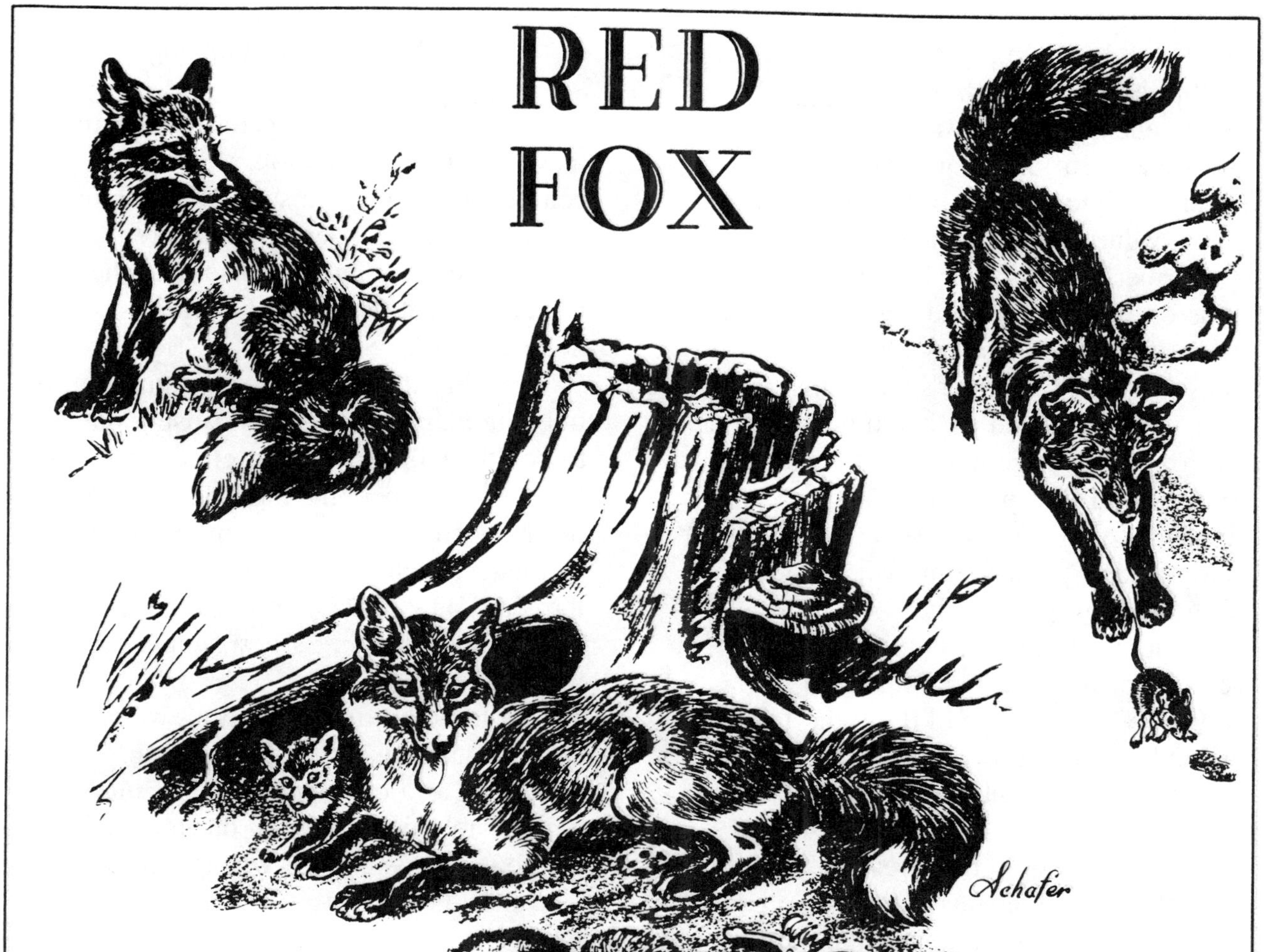
RED
FOX
Schafer

exactly to his liking and he thrives, multiplies, and finds himself listed as a public enemy by some farmers and sportsmen. But, more and more, the general public appears to becoming aware of the value of such animals.

Farmers are enraged by his occasional raids on the poultry yard, and sportsmen by his fondness for a luscious pheasant or juicy rabbit. The farmer's anger may be somewhat mitigated by his knowledge that the fox eats a large number of small rodents, and the sportsman's anger somewhat mollified by the fact that he can enjoy a fox hunt at a time when no other form of hunting is legal.

In some states, fox hunting is taken very seriously as a traditional sport. Anyone who suggested killing the fox at the end of the chase would be socially ostracized, if not actually subjected to bodily injury.

Many hunters in the Great Lakes region class the red fox as our number one game animal. There is little doubt that the fox deserves this respect. Sportsmen who enjoy hearing a well-trained pack of hounds in "full cry" can find few quarries as well qualified to lead the pack. Even at the end of the day, the red fox is usually well out in front, and many hunters swear he enjoys the chase, too.

Thus, it may be seen that the red fox has his friends as well as his enemies, and that a very careful audit indeed must be made if a true balance sheet is to be made out for him. He is obviously no paragon of virtue, but neither is he a perfidious wretch without redeeming features. Like most of us, he has his good points and his bad ones, and is cast now as a hero, then as a villain, dependent on local circumstances and the particular viewpoint of his accuser or defender.

Is No Wizard of Cunning

When foxes are comparatively scarce they attract little attention, and consequently, little censure. When foxes are abundant their depredations are naturally more numerous also, and they receive a great deal of unfavorable notoriety.

Probably the common sense program of trapping and hunting foxes causing damage to poultry will prove most effective in the long run. Trappers have proven that the red fox is not the wizard of cunning that fable and legend indicate, and that any farmer or farmer's son can trap the foxes in his locality by following a few simple instructions.

Perhaps the time is coming when we can consider the fox without bias or prejudice, as a component part of our wildlife mosaic, and work out logical methods for his control when control is advisable.

Red Fox

Vulpes vulpes

Size:	8-16 pounds
Range:	Throughout the Great Lakes region.
Habitat:	A mix of woods and open fields. Does not thrive in unbroken forests.
Fact:	The red fox is highly adaptable and can be found in suburban areas.

The Lynx and Bobcat-- *Cats of the Wild North*

While most of the cat family scattered over the world have long tails and rounded ears, the big wildcats of North America have short tails and tufted ears.

Lynx and bobcat are much larger than domestic cats but far inferior to the really big cats like the lion, tiger, leopard, and jaguar. Both have short bodies, very short tails, long heavy limbs, bearded cheeks, and tufted ears.

Lynx and bobcat are sometimes confused in the wild, and observers occasionally mistake a big bobcat for a lynx. The lynx has the tip of the tail entirely black above and below, the rest of the tail being grayish white.

The bobcat has the tip of the tail black above and white below, with broken bars of color on the upper part of the tail.

The animals also differ in the feet, since the feet of the lynx are much larger, and look huge, due to their hairy development. They function in winter as snowshoes, enabling the big lynx to walk over snow in which a dog of approximately equal weight would flounder helplessly.

The lynx is pale grayish in color, without dark spots, while the bobcat is brownish, with spots or cloudy places all over the body. An adult lynx is also considerably heavier than an adult bobcat. While both the true lynx, generally called Canada lynx; and the bobcat, sometimes call the bay lynx, occurred commonly in the Great Lakes region at one time, the Canada lynx is rarely found in the U.S. at the present time although there is evidence that a population comeback may be occurring. The bobcat, however, is still common, and bobcat hunting is a winter sport in many northern areas.

The comparative scarcity of the lynx in the region is probably due to his liking for dense forests. As the primitive forests were cut, the lynx retreated north, and now is found chiefly in the vast forested region north of Lake Superior. The bobcat, which prefers tangles, thickets, and cutover brush lands in deep forests, may actually increase following the lumbermen.

Lynx is Patient Hunter

The lynx, as might be expected from a forest dweller, is extremely agile among logs and branches, and a splendid leaper, but not a good runner on the ground. He captures his prey largely through skill and patience, and seldom attempts to run anything down. He is less cunning than the fox, but more patient; less powerful than the wolf, but a better jumper and even more resistant to famine.

The lynx, as might be expected from a forest dweller, is extremely agile among logs and branches.

The lynx attacks with a tremendous leap, and if this misses, he is likely to return to his crouching place to wait patiently for another possible victim. In addition to his habitual fare of snowshoe hares, the lynx kills grouse, squirrels, and curiously enough, foxes. This is quite a reversal of the usual "dog chase cat" situation, but is well known in the north country.

In times of deep snow, foxes are unable to escape by speed, and are soon overtaken and devoured by the powerful lynx on his snowshoe feet.

In times of deep snow, foxes are unable to escape by speed, and are soon overtaken and devoured by the powerful lynx.

Lynx also occasionally kill deer when pressed by hunger, although this seems to be unusual. Of course, a hungry lynx is not particular and will tackle most anything he thinks he can overcome. Even porcupines are attacked and killed at such times, but the lynx usually dies from the terrible effect of the quills later on.

There is no evidence that a lynx will attack a man, although they were much feared in pioneer days. Two facts seem to have accounted for this fear of the lynx. A lynx will sometimes follow a man through the woods, either parallel or just behind. This seems to be from sheer curiosity, as such a performance never results in an attack.

Secondly, and perhaps more significant, the lynx has an appalling cry. This cry, uttered at night in the lonely wilderness, affects people very strongly, and it seems hard for a person to believe that a big cat which screams like that is anything but a terrible enemy. The lynx is apparently one of those creatures who inspire terror because of a big voice and a bad reputation.

Bobcat Continues to Thrive

Although the lynx turns up only now and then in the Great Lakes region, the bobcat is very much with us. It has been aptly said that the lynx is a cat of the big timber and Canadian climate, while the bobcat is a cat of the little timber and United States climate.

As the big timber of the Great Lakes region was cleared away, the lynx all but disappeared, but the bobcat thrived. Only when the clearing process is carried to the ultimate of agricultural land with little timber of any kind does the bobcat disappear also.

Perhaps the simple childish description of the bobcat as a "great big pussycat with a bob tail" is the best which can be offered. The savage wildness of the big eyes, and the incessant nervous twitching of the short tail distinguish it from its domestic cousins, however.

In the wild, the bobcat is probably an animal with a small range. A thousand acres or so of dense cover, with a good supply of food, would presumably suffice for a bobcat, except during the courting season, when, like all cats, he goes out on the prowl.

In the wild, the bobcat is probably an animal with a small range.

The den is made in a hollow tree or log, and lined with leaves or moss. Mating takes place in late winter or early spring, and from two to four young are born about 70 days later. The kittens resemble domestic kittens, and are blind and helpless at birth. They are as cute and playful as any kittens, and are carried by the neck just like domestic kittens.

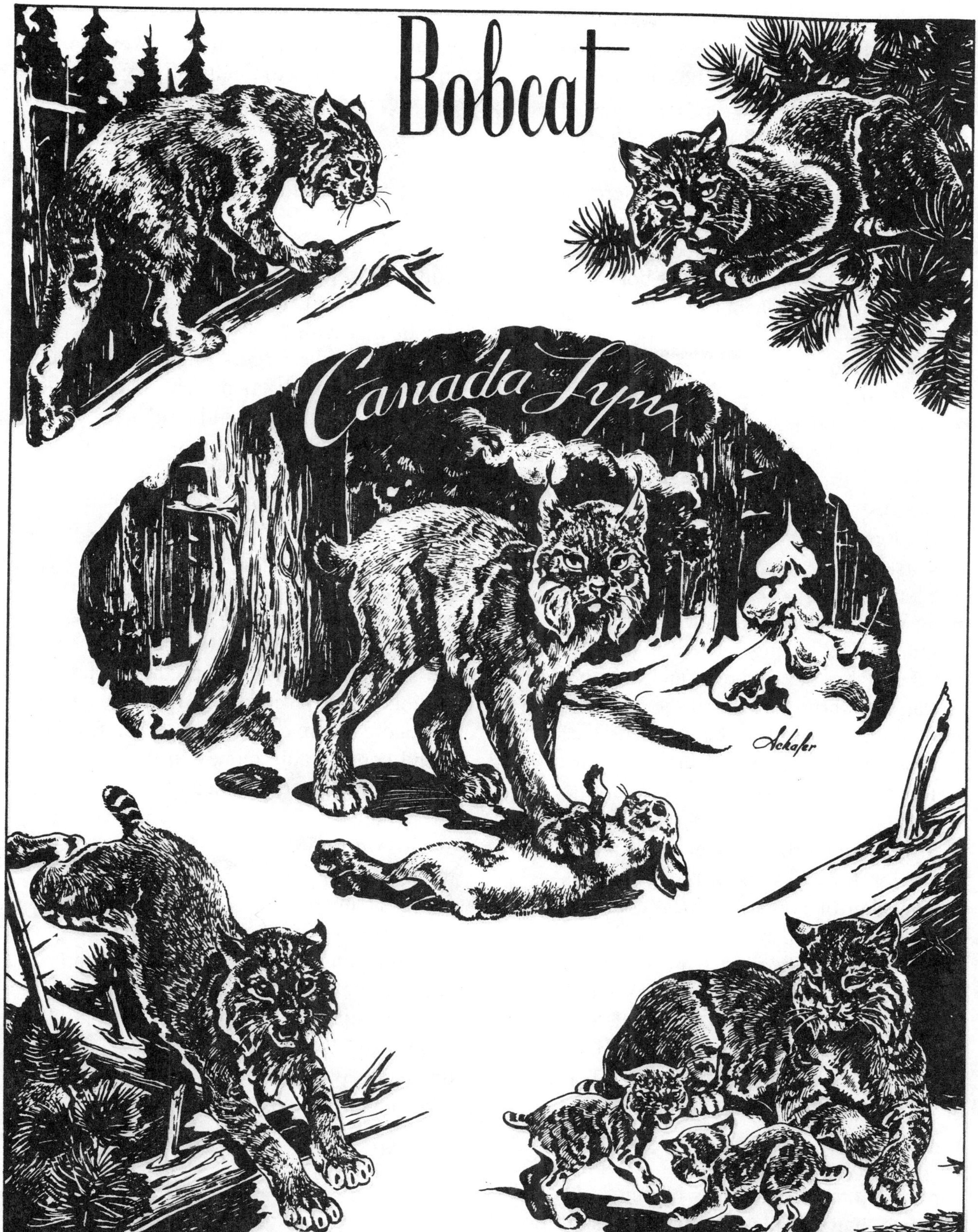
Bobcat
Canada Lynx
Schafer

Bobcats purr, meow, and screech like housecats, but louder. The bobcat is essentially a hunter, and prefers to catch his own prey, although it is not averse to eating dead animals killed by others.

While most of his prey is smaller than himself, he is extremely courageous, and sometimes tackles pretty good-sized animals. There is no doubt that bobcats occasionally kill deer, but this is a rare event. Mice, squirrels, rabbits, hares, grouse, small birds, and eggs of every sort are the staple food of bobcats.

There is no doubt that bobcats occasionally kill deer.

Seldom do bobcats supplement their menu with delectable dainties such as poultry, lambs, or pigs. There is always that detestable odor of man and dog to be met around farm yards, and the danger of guns, trap, or poison to be avoided. The bobcat is a shy fellow at heart, and much prefers to keep out of sight and out of trouble.

It is claimed that the best possible protection for chickens or other poultry roosting out of doors in bobcat country is a flock of guineas. No matter what the hour of day or night, the alert guineas start up that infernal racket for which they are famous, or notorious, and the startled bobcat flees precipitately to the nearest thicket to calm his jangled nerves. Then he prowls away in search of less noisy victims.

A newly caught bobcat is a diabolical appearing creature, its eyes blazing defiance, hair rumpled, teeth bared, spitting fury at all who approach closely. When captured very young, and treated gently, they sometimes become as quiet and playful as house cats. Often, however, even tiny bobcats are little balls of fury, biting, clawing, and snarling at their would be tamers.

Has Value as Sporting Animal

Certainly, making a pet of a bobcat requires the patience of Job and the gentleness of St. Frances, and even if one is endowed with their attributes, a little insurance on the fingers might be in order. Overall, it is not a good idea to attempt to tame bobcats--or any wild animal.

Bobcat hunting is becoming a headline sport in parts of the northern Great Lakes, and attracts many hunters from urban areas. Since resort owners and others in the home range of the bobcat cannot rely solely on hunting and fishing to attract tourism, the addition of bobcat hunts is appealing. Winter sports are few in these areas, and the hunting of predatory animals such as the coyote, fox, and bobcat are of decided economic importance. Hunters spend considerable money in the course of these hunts, most of it near the location of the hunt.

So, we find that the bobcat has finally acquired local friends, who see him as an economic asset to the community instead of just an untamed savage who ought to be exterminated.

We find that the bobcat has finally acquired local friends.

Lynx
Lynx canadensis

Size: 11 to 37 pounds
Range: Michigan's Upper Peninsula, northern Wisconsin and Minnesota, and Ontario.
Habitat: Undisturbed coniferous forests, including both upland and wetland forests.
Fact: The snowshoe hare is the preferred fare and lynx can live as long as 15 years in the wild although most live only 4 or 5.

Bobcat
Lynx rufus

Size: 11 to 35 pounds
Range: Ontario, northern Michigan, including northern lower Michigan, much of Wisconsin and Minnesota.
Habitat: Prefers large tracts of forests and seems to frequently inhabit woodlots near rivers.
Fact: The bobcat is generally a loner. It sometimes lives up to 12 years in the wild.

The Woodchuck--
Professional Excavator

The woodchuck is known by many local names, among the best known being ground hog, whistle pig, and eastern marmot.

As indicated by its scientific name, *Marmota monax*, the woodchuck is a member of the widely distributed marmot clan, and is actually a big, clumsy ground dwelling member of the *Sciuridae*, or squirrel family.

It seems somewhat odd to associate the small-tailed, heavy bodied, burrow-digging woodchuck with the large-tailed, slender, tree-climbing fox or red squirrel, but if we remember also the various chipmunks, gophers, and ground squirrels, the transition is easier to understand. The woodchuck occasionally reminds us rather sharply of his squirrel ancestry by climbing a tree to escape dogs or to keep a better lookout over his home territory.

Woodchucks Typical Hibernators

Although the habitat of the eastern woodchuck, which we have in the Great Lakes region, differs widely from that of the western marmots of the great mountains, their habits are remarkably similar. The marmots are all vegetarians, all live in burrows, all stay pretty close to home, all tend to whistle sharply when surprised, and all go into winter hibernation.

Woodchucks may be called typical hibernators, or winter sleepers. When the temperature begins to drop in late fall, about November in this region, the woodchuck, fast as a Thanksgiving turkey, crawls down into his underground hole, pulls the hole in after him by caving in the dirt in the passage to the next, and goes to sleep for the winter.

During this period of hibernation, nothing is eaten so that no fuel is received to be converted into bodily heat by the oxidation of the blood through breathing; on the contrary, the lungs almost cease to work. There is an occasional respiration--a sighing inhalation of breath--but most of the time the only oxygen in the lungs is the trifle reaching them by the slow heart beats, and by the diffusion of gases. A mirror held before the mouth and nostrils is not clouded by breath. The animal may be placed under water, or in a jar of carbonic acid gas, for an hour or more, without drowning or suffocating; nevertheless, respiration and other bodily functions do not entirely cease.

What, then, supplies the meager warmth required? It is the slow absorption and combustion of the fat stored up under the skin by the abundant feeding of summer and fall. This is shown also by the fact that when the animals emerge in spring, they are thin and weak, as contrasted with their strength and fatness when they started hibernation.

Their awakening must be gentle and gradual, as the sudden forcible arousing of hibernators often causes death. Here, a curious fact may be mentioned: in spite of their comatose condition, which has been likened to human beings in a state of trance, they are sensitive to the slightest touch; merely blowing on the hair will induce an instant response, although not in the least arousing the sleeper. The period of hibernation varies not only with different kinds of animals, but with the same kinds under different or even similar conditions.

That this winter sleep is of a highly protective character cannot be doubted, since the true hibernators are those whose food fails altogether in winter, and is of such a nature that it cannot be stored up in sufficient quantity.

Winter sleep is of a highly protective character.

Contrary to tradition, woodchucks in the Great Lakes region do not emerge from their winter sleep promptly at sunrise of February 2 to watch for their shadows on the snow or earth as the case may be. They do seem to become restless and awaken more and more frequently during late winter and early spring, finally coming out to stay when the snow is gone and tender shoots are starting in the fields.

The mating season is believed to be in late March, and the young are born in late April or early May. Very small and undeveloped at birth, probably blind for about a month, they do not venture from the den until they are six or seven weeks old. They begin to eat solid food in the form of grass and clover as soon as they are able to get out to find it. The mother, or both parents, attend them carefully at first, showing them where and when to eat, as well as some of the dangers of the outside world.

At times, the young and adventurous woodchucks cause damage to gardens and truck patches. As the end of August approaches the animals are nearly full grown, and scatter to dig homes of their own.

May Dig Fifty-Foot Burrows

Woodchuck burrows may be found in woods or fields, but perhaps the most favored location is at the edge of a woodlot or swale adjoining a field of clover or alfalfa. One entrance to the burrow is marked by a heap of dirt thrown out during the excavation, but one or more other entrances without external evidences are often present also. These concealed openings are used as lookouts or spy holes, and here the woodchuck watches intruders whose attention may be attracted by the obvious pile of dirt, while the woodchuck himself remains undetected.

The length of the burrow varies according to the type of soil and surface topography. The total length may be somewhere between seven and 50 feet, and the depth up to six or seven feet.

The length of the burrow varies according to the type of soil and surface topography.

Disease does not seem to play a prominent part in the life history of woodchucks, since there is no record of plague or epidemic, and few woodchucks have been found dead from disease or parasitic infection. Man, dogs, and foxes are probably his chief enemies in the order stated, although hawks may occasionally get a young woodchuck during its first

WOODCHUCK

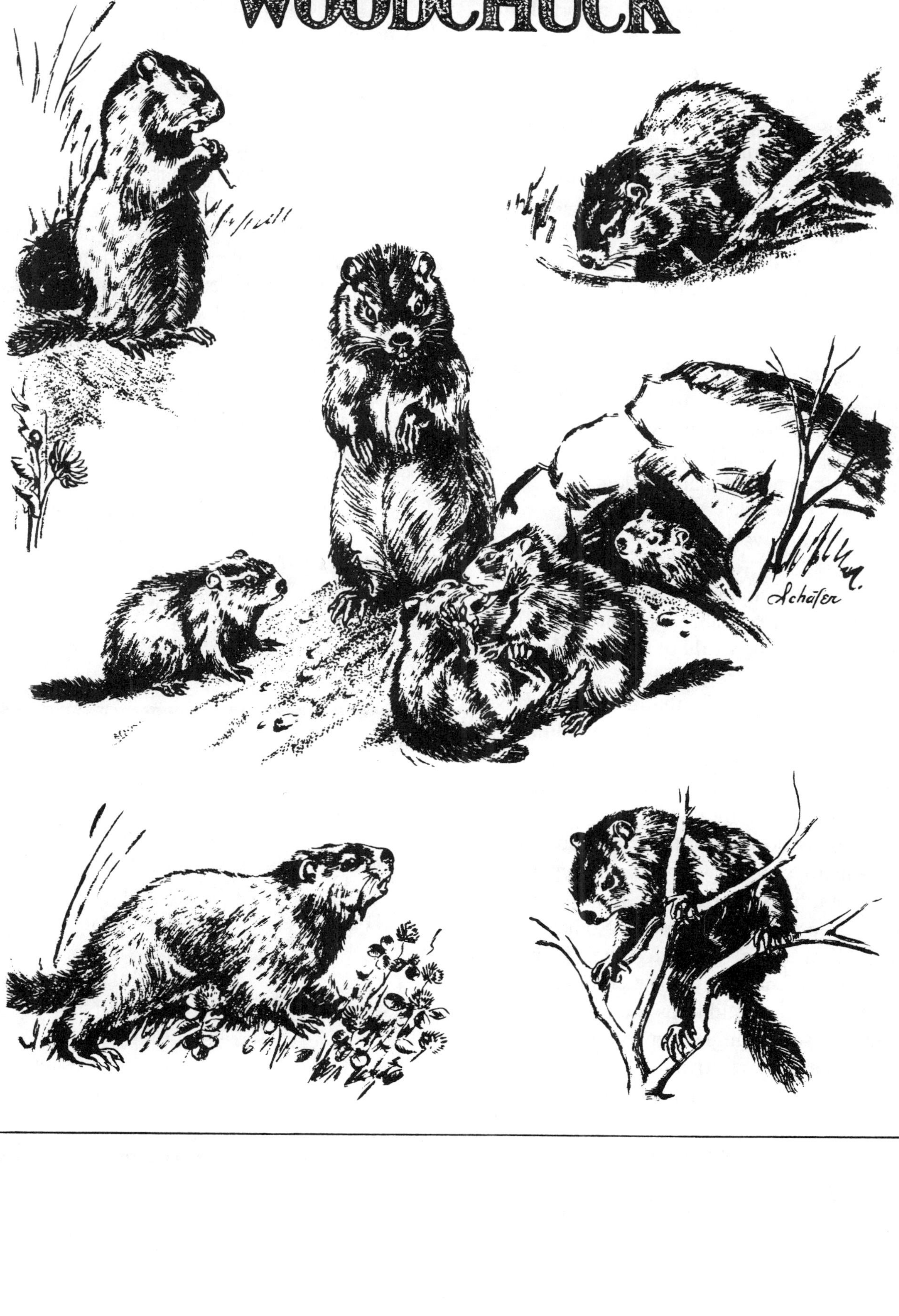

days above ground.

Red foxes and badgers are reported to dig out woodchucks under certain circumstances, although this is probably not a common occurrence.

While young woodchucks are good to eat, and sometimes are eaten by farmers and sportsmen, the primary economic importance of the woodchuck lies in his digging propensities. Farmers do not like the heaps of dirt piled up by the woodchuck at the entrance to his den in clover and alfalfa fields, nor the concealed almost vertical hole used as a lookout. The cutter bars of mowers are dulled and the blades nicked in the dirt. Occasionally a farm horse broke or twisted his leg by stepping in a "chuck hole." Nowadays, tractors don't have that problem.

Burrows Help Other Wildlife

The other side of the woodchuck hole situation, and probably the more important one, is the value of these holes as dens and refuges for other wildlife. Some wildlife investigators maintain that numbers and distribution of the woodchuck are among the more important ecological factors influencing the numbers and distribution of the cottontail rabbit.

Rabbits do not dig their own burrows, or construct their own hiding places. Old farm buildings, brush piles, junk heaps, stone piles and the burrows of other animals are their only safe retreats, and man has a tendency toward eliminating many of these. Buildings are razed, brushpiles and tangled fence rows burned, and stone piles removed.

Farmers kill woodchucks because of real or fancied damage, and sportsmen kill them because they like that type of hunting, which the woodchuck offers. All these things together are likely to add up to less cottontail rabbits.

The recognized importance of the woodchuck as a game animal and a provider of dens for cottontails has brought about a change of public opinion and a change in the legal status of the animals.

No counties now offer bounties for woodchuck scalps, formerly a common practice.

Woodchucks are given legal protection in many Great Lakes states and may be taken only during certain seasons. Since woodchucks are in hibernation during most of the period after late October, this, in effect, closes the season to woodchuck hunting. Farmers are allowed to kill woodchucks doing damage on their property at any time.

In recent years, woodchucks have been holding their own after making a comeback in numbers as compared to their scarcity in the late 1930's.

Woodchuck
Marmota monax

Size:	5 to 11 pounds
Range:	Throughout the Great Lakes region.
Habitat:	Small woodlots, brushy fencelines, open pastureland.
Fact:	May live up to six years in the wild although most do not live beyond three.

The Lesser Squirrels--
Curious Critters of the Wild

In addition to the big three game squirrels--fox, gray, and black--we have in the Great Lakes region several species of smaller squirrels, no less interesting, but perhaps less well known.

Red Squirrel

One of these "lesser squirrels" is the red squirrel, which looks very much like his larger cousin, the fox squirrel. Its habits are also much the same.

The red squirrel is considerably smaller than the fox squirrel, with a little more red in his coat, and may be distinguished also by a black line along the side between the white belly and the reddish upper parts.

Apparently red squirrels compete with both fox and gray squirrels for food and territory when they happen to inhabit the same woods. Red squirrels are very active and noisy; and so belligerent that they attack the bigger fox squirrels without hesitation, and usually chase them off the field of battle.

Nuts form their staple food, but seeds, berries, fruits, roots, fungi, insects, and grubs, worms, pine cones, and almost everything edible to be found are eaten during the course of the year. The red squirrel has quite a taste for meat, and robs birds' nests and mouse nests when eggs or small young are present.

Chipmunk

Still smaller than red squirrels, and somewhat different in habits, are the chipmunks. Chipmunks may be recognized by their small size, by the three dark and two light stripes on the side of the face, and the five dark and four light stripes on the back and sides.

Chipmunks are dwellers in forest and brush lands but are found on or near the ground more often than in the tree tops. They are more provident than are the larger tree squirrels, and store quantities of food in underground granaries. All sorts of seeds, nuts, fruits, and insects are eaten and supplies of these viands are lugged in the capacious cheek pouches to the subterranean storehouses.

Chipmunks are hermits by nature, and live solitary lives except during the breeding season. Two litters are usually produced annually, with from two to eight young per litter. Chipmunks are cute little fellows and often become tame enough to eat out of the hand.

Like red squirrels, they are of little economic importance. There are two species that inhabit the region. The least chipmunk is found in northern areas of the Great Lakes region and the eastern chipmunk, which inhabits much of the region.

Striped Ground Squirrel

This little rodent is also known in the Great Lakes region as the thirteen-lined spermophile and the gopher. Neither of these latter names is a suitable one. In the first place, the animal does not have thirteen stripes, but 23--12 dark ones and 11 light ones. In the next place, the word "spermophile" means "seed lover," and while these animals do eat seeds, so do most other rodents.

The term "gopher," perhaps most commonly used in the region, is really a localism, and would be misleading to people from outside the area. In the south, gopher means a type of small burrowing land tortoise common in that region.

The term "gopher," perhaps most commonly used in the region, is really a localism.

In the west, the term is applied loosely to all ground dwelling squirrels, but particularly to the odd group of pocket gophers, which are not found in this region at all. It so happens that in the Great Lakes region we have but one ground squirrel, while in many states there are various species, and even several genera, of ground squirrels. So the term "gopher" lacks significance, and it is better to call our animal the striped ground squirrel.

Our ground squirrel lives in open fields and grasslands, where he digs his little burrows. The burrows are much like miniature woodchuck burrows, and we should keep in mind that woodchucks are merely big ground squirrels after all.

Ground squirrels hibernate in winter, again showing their kinship to the woodchuck. They retire to their underground dens in September or October, and emerge in March or April, thus escaping winter altogether. This is the cheapest and easiest method of dodging cold weather ever devised; simpler and less dangerous than the migration of birds, and perhaps someday members of the human race may find a way of utilizing a similar scheme.

Young are produced in late spring or early summer, from six or seven to a dozen per litter. They are naked and blind at birth, open their eyes nearly a month later, and are usually five or six weeks old when they first emerge from the den.

Our ground squirrels are of little economic importance, since they seldom become really abundant; their burrows are too small to be a nuisance except on lawns or golf courses. The grubs and insects they consume probably compensate for the grain taken from crop lands.

Their western relations, however, cannot be so readily dismissed, for they are far more abundant, and many species are much larger in size. Also, many of the western ground squirrels are colonial in habit, and a colony may be very destructive to crops, while on steep slopes their many burrows may lead to soil erosion.

Extensive rodent control campaigns have been carried on in western states to rid lands of ground squirrels.

Biologists point out that some of these extensive, and expensive, campaigns would not have been necessary had not previous campaigns greatly reduced the natural enemies of the ground squirrels. Wolves, coyotes, foxes, hawks, owls, etc., the predators whose natural function is to hold in check the rodent populations, are ruthlessly cut down under the guise of "vermin control."

A little more foresight in preserving the balance of nature would sometimes save the cost of expensive "control campaigns" later on.

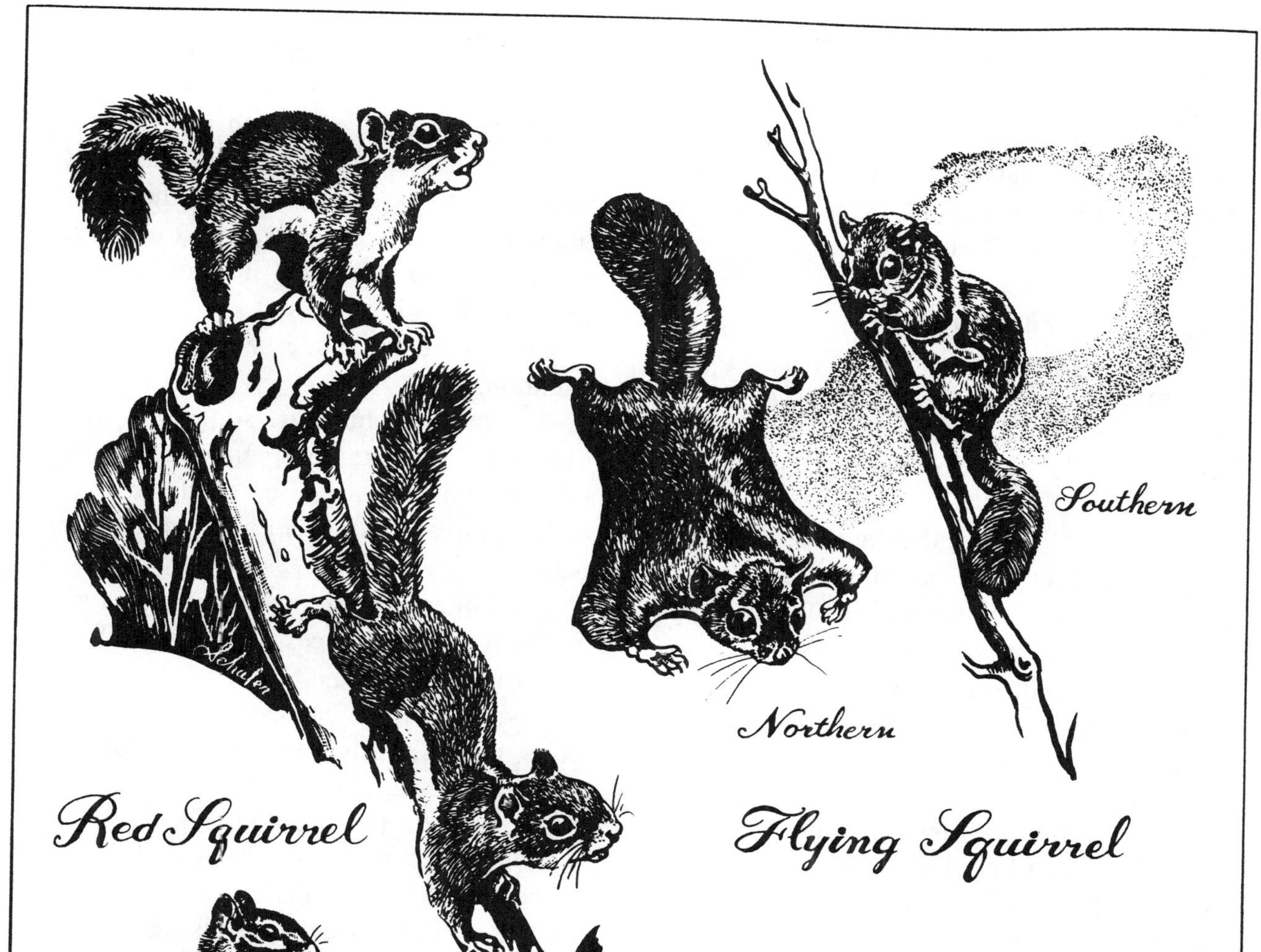
Red Squirrel
Northern
Southern
Flying Squirrel
Eastern
Least
Chipmunk
Striped Spermophile
Schafer

And the rodent populations expand like steam from a teakettle when the lid is removed. A little more foresight in preserving the balance of nature would sometimes save the cost of expensive "control campaigns" later on.

Flying Squirrel

Perhaps the most interesting and at the same time most inconspicuous of the Great Lakes squirrels are the so-called flying squirrels.

Actually, of course, they are not flyers, but gliders. They have no wings, and cannot maintain themselves in the air. Gliding is accomplished by means of a loose fold of skin which extends from the outside of the wrist to the hind foot. When the legs are spread, the entire under surface and skin attachment form a flat plane well adapted for gliding through the air.

The flattened tail is an additional aid in gliding and in steering. The best description of their gliding flight is that quoted by Seton: "Occasionally, in the evening twilight or on moonlight nights, a flying squirrel may be seen sailing in a gentle downward curve from one tree to another, the start being made from well toward the top of one tree and the place of alighting at a much lower point on the other. There is something ghostlike in this gliding flight. It is so unlike that of any other of our native creatures. There is not only an entire absence of fluttering wings, but complete silence."

The flattened tail is an additional aid in gliding and in steering.

The distance covered in a glide depends upon the height of launching and that of landing, but seldom exceeds a hundred feet.

Flying squirrels are found in wooded areas throughout the region but since they are our only nocturnal squirrels, they are seldom seen. Occasionally one is captured when a hollow tree is cut in winter, and the beautiful silky fur, soft grayish brown above and creamy white below, attracts attention.

The little creatures are sometimes kept as pets for they are very gentle and readily take to being handled. But, as stated earlier, the wild is not a good place to find pets.

Two litters of from two to six young are born in hollow trees or leaf nests from May to August.

Flying squirrels eat seeds, buds, nuts, fruits, insects, birds' eggs, and possibly young birds, since they have a decidedly carnivorous turn of appetite. Their economic importance is practically nil, due to their small size and limited numbers. Two species of flying squirrels--the northern and southern--are found in the Great Lakes region with the northern being somewhat larger of the two.

Red Squirrel

Tamiasciurus hudsonicus

Size: 4.8 to 8.8 ounces
Range: Found throughout the Great Lakes region except rare in Illinois.
Habitat: Prefers mixed coniferous and hardwood woodlots.

Chipmunk
Tamias striatus

Size: 2.3 to 4.1 ounces
Range: Throughout the Great Lakes region.
Habitat: The chipmunk prefers mature, open deciduous forests.
Fact: When startled, the chipmunk emits a squeak that sounds much like a bird.

Flying Squirrel (Southern)
Glaucomys volans

Size: 1.8 to 2.6 ounces
Range: Most of the Great Lakes region except rare north such as Michigan's Upper Peninsula. There, the northern flying squirrel is found.
Habitat: Open hardwood forests with some thickets.
Fact: These squirrels glide, not fly. They can be attracted to peanut butter at night.

Striped Ground Squirrel
Spermophilus tridecemlineatus

Size: 3.5 to 7.8 ounces
Range: Western Great Lakes region, including most of Michigan, and states west.
Habitat: This squirrel prefers grasslands and avoids woodlots.
Fact: This species is semi-colonial and may live in small groups.

The Game Squirrels--
Fox, Gray, and Black

The family name of these squirrels--*Sciuridae*--means "shade-tailed." It is a name appropriate enough when we think of their long bushy tails, which curve so gracefully over the back and form a warm blanket when the animal is curled up asleep. All this group of squirrels are similarly agile, alert, curious, noisy, and full of business.

Squirrels inhabit hollows in trunks of trees, make globular nests of leafy twigs in lofty branches, and spend most of their lives aloft.

Nuts form their staple food, but berries, fruits, grains, fungi, insects and their grubs, etc., offer variations in the menu at different seasons. Carnivorous tastes also occur among the squirrels, and these little meddlers often get into traps baited with meat for martens, skunks, raccoons, etc.

Some squirrels rob birds' nests, and may even kill small birds and mammals. The saucy little red squirrel, however, is more apt to get into this sort of mischief than are the larger squirrels described here.

Nuts form their staple food, but berries, fruits, grains, fungi, insects and their grubs, etc., offer variations in the menu at different seasons.

Although we speak of three squirrels, fox, gray, and black, there are really only two of them, since black squirrels are merely a color variation of the gray species, and black and gray young may occur in the same litter, just as black kittens occur in a litter with other color phases.

This fact is not well understood and has even led to confusing hunting seasons.

Gray squirrels may be distinguished from fox squirrels by their smaller size, white under parts and the white edging of the tail. Some fox squirrels tend toward a grayish color, and the difference in size may not be readily apparent from some distance. This is especially true if the animals are partially concealed in foliage. Black specimens occur among fox squirrels, but they are not as common as they are among gray species. Albino individuals--pure white--also appear occasionally among squirrels.

While there is some overlapping of range between fox and gray squirrels, they do not coincide, since the preferred habitat of the two differs. The gray squirrel is essentially a creature of the big timber, where plenty of nuts and deep shade prevail. The fox squirrel prefers more open country, with a more varied food supply. Fox squirrels are more adaptable than are gray squirrels, and maintain their numbers much better in the presence of agriculture.

When the pioneer farmers settled in the Great Lakes region, they found gray squirrels plentiful, and fox squirrels scarce or absent. As farms increased in number and acreage, fox squirrels increased and gray squirrels decreased so that most of the southern areas of the region are now well populated with fox squirrels, while grays are practically gone.

In northern areas, the gray squirrel still holds his own, although fox squirrels seem to be gaining in certain locations. Gray squirrels, especially the handsome black variation, are still to be found in some southern cities and parks, where they are much admired and protected from human interference.

Mating, gestation period, and litter numbers are similar in fox and gray squirrels. Two litters per year are often produced, the first coming in March, the second in mid-summer.

Young vary in number from one to six, three being the average litter. Old females ordinarily breed twice a year and yearling females but once. Juveniles are dependent on the mother for about three months. Young are born either in hollow trees or in leafy nests, depending partly on the weather and the availability of suitable trees.

Young vary in number from one to six, three being the average litter.

Squirrels are subject to diseases and parasites, like other mammals, and perhaps the disease known as mange or scabies is most important of these. This disease appears just about every year, but in some years seems much more virulent than in others.

The characteristic symptom of mange is a loss of hair. This may affect only a small part of the animal or may result in a "hairless" squirrel. If a high percentage of the skin is affected, the animal is likely to die.

The disease is caused by a mite (not an insect but a relative of the spider) which burrows in the skin, causing the hair to fall out and scabs to form. An epidemic of mange is more likely to occur when squirrels are most abundant, and consequently most likely to contact each other or to contact nests already infested.

Since we cannot run squirrels through a dipping tank as we do cattle or sheep in similar circumstances, there is little or nothing to be done for them. Experience with all species of animals, including man, indicates that when populations are high, with much over-crowding, epidemics are likely to develop.

Probably more important than the actual deaths from mange is the weakening of the infected squirrels, leaving them more susceptible to cold and wet, and more easily caught by their enemies while in search of food.

Squirrels Do Not Hibernate

Since high squirrel populations frequently result in disease and winter starvation, it appears to be good conservation to reduce such populations before winter sets in, and the simplest way to do this is to harvest the surplus crop during the fall hunting season.

Unlike some of the squirrel family, such as the woodchuck, chipmunk, and many ground squirrels, the game squirrels do not go into hibernation in winter. They can and do remain in their holes for some days during extreme cold and storm, but they must emerge to obtain food after a short period of inaction.

Neither have they developed a system of food storage like certain rodents of western North America and Asia and others that actually stock their winter food

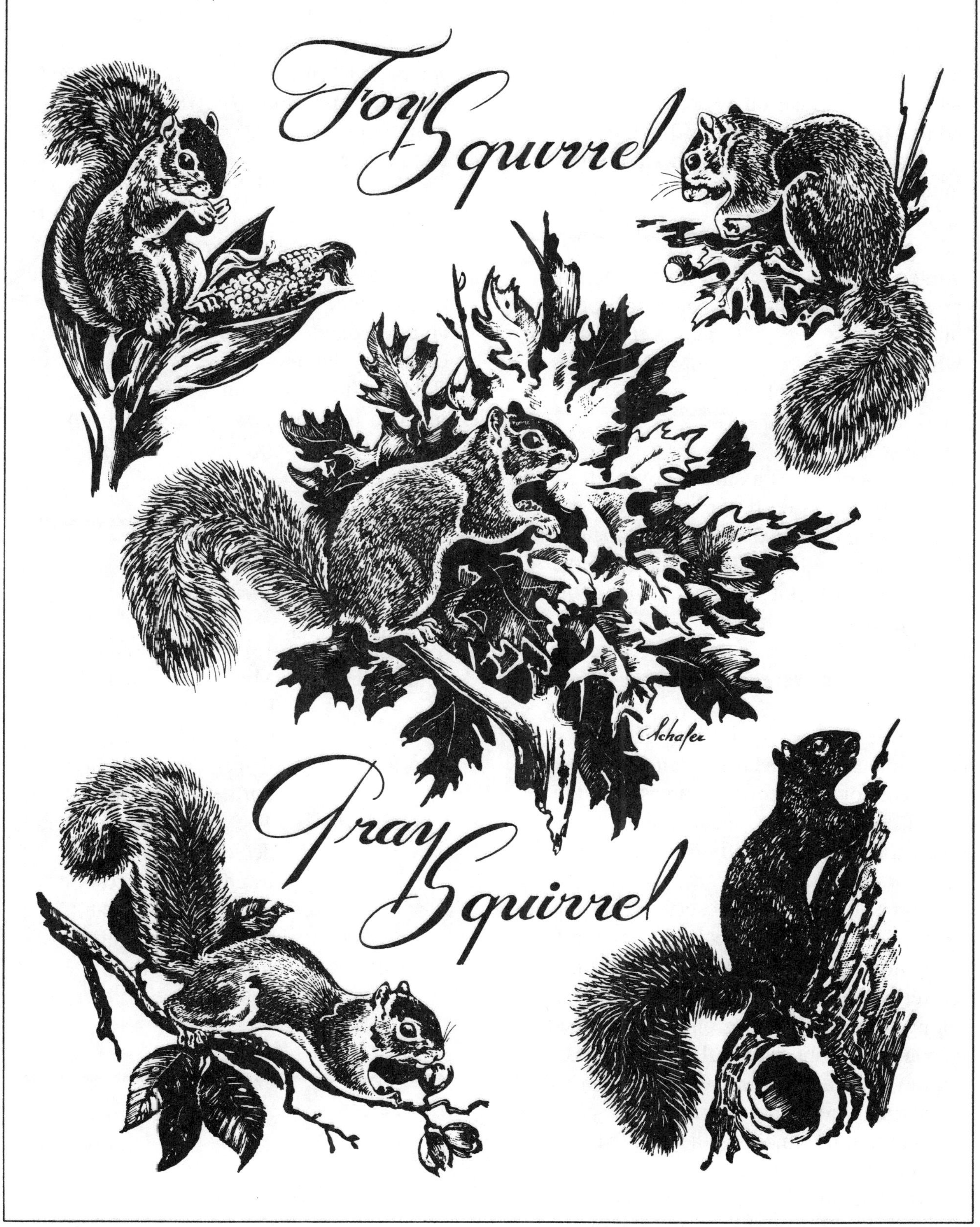
Fox Squirrel
Schafer
Gray Squirrel

supply in summer and fall. Our squirrels have gone part way in food storage by burying nuts all over their home range, which they industriously search out for winter food.

A single squirrel may hide more than a thousand nuts, and if he finds them all, should make out all right for the winter. It is, however, a moot question as to whether a squirrel finds all or most of these hidden nuts, and just how he locates them under a snowy cover. It is generally supposed that a combination of memory and sense of smell are called into play, but it is also unlikely that even the smartest and luckiest ever finds all of his hidden treasure.

A single squirrel may hide more than a thousand nuts.

Once Were Great Travelers

While at present we think of our squirrels as permanent residents in our woodlots or local forested areas, in primitive times, they seem to have been great travelers with definite migratory tendencies.

According to early observers, gray squirrels undertook mass migrations in the fall, moving in thousands, generally in an easterly or southerly direction. They moved along leisurely, feeding on nuts and seeds enroute, and unhesitatingly swam creeks and even rivers as they were encountered.

Farmers regarded them with consternation, almost as they regard a plague of locusts or grasshoppers today, for they created havoc in corn fields or grain fields. Thousands of squirrels were killed by farmers armed with clubs and stones. There seems to be some doubt as to where the migrations originated, how far the animals traveled, or where they ended since communications were largely non-existent in those early days, and observations were necessarily casual and uncorrelated.

Very likely a high percentage of the migrating animals perished enroute. Such large scale migrations seem to be a thing of the past, and are almost incredible to us today. Since the migrations took place in autumn, they could hardly have been caused by famine; there are no records of flood or fire to account for them. We are inclined to think they must have been caused by overpopulation.

Fox Squirrel
Sciurus niger

Size:	1.5 to 2.5 pounds
Range:	Most of the Great Lakes region except Ontario, Michigan's Upper Peninsula and northern Wisconsin.
Habitat:	The fox squirrel prefers deciduous forests. Regenerated forests of the southern Great Lakes region are ideal.
Fact:	Rarely seen in the "black phase."

Gray Squirrel
Sciurus carolinensis

Size: .75 to 1.75 pounds
Range: Throughout the Great Lakes region except rare in Ontario.
Habitat: The gray squirrel prefers mature deciduous forests but can also be found in parks and residential neighborhoods.
Fact: The black phase of this squirrel is often referred to as the "black squirrel" although they are one and the same animal.

The Beaver--
Engineer of the Wilds

Perhaps no other North American mammal has given rise to so many stories or to so voluminous literature as has the beaver. Many researchers have written about the manifold details of the beaver's life and its feats of engineering.

In addition to its interesting habits and anatomy, the beaver played an important role in the exploration and early settlement of North America. It was because of the beaver that Nicolet first visited the Straits of Michillmackinac in 1635 and an influx of settlers followed two centuries later.

In 1660 Radisson and Groseilliers returned to Montreal after 18 months in the wilds of what would later be called Michigan, bringing with them 60 canoes laden with nearly a quarter of a million dollars worth of fur.

Fashion's whim had elevated the beaver hat to a position of exalted importance. The "wolf" of the time, whether young man about town, dignified banker, or big butter and egg man, could hardly ply his trade without a beaver hat to crown his wardrobe.

Fashion's whim had elevated the beaver hat to a position of exalted importance.

Huge companies were formed, and wars were fought to control the trade in beaver pelts. For 250 years the Hudson's Bay Company held despotic sway over most of Canada, and some great American fortunes of today have their roots in the fur trade of early times.

Skins Once Stable Currency

At times, beaver skins were stable currency for half a continent. With the substitution of silk fiber for beaver fur in hats and the simultaneous exhaustion of the easily available fur supply, the devotees of fashion turned to other fads. The beaver lost its prominent position in the fur trade.

The long exploitation by fur traders brought about a decline in beaver population and range, accentuated by the high price levels during and immediately following World War I. In 1920, it was found necessary to impose an extended closed season on beaver trapping in much of the Great Lakes region to preserve the few beavers still remaining in remote or sparsely settled areas. By 1931, beaver had become sufficiently abundant so that open seasons were again authorized, and these seasons have continued, with various modifications, to the present time.

The beaver is a rodent, looking somewhat like a giant muskrat except for his flat, trowel-like tail.

He is the largest rodent in North America, and the second largest rodent in the world, surpassed only by the capybara of South America. An adult beaver weighs from 40 to 70 pounds, with a few outsize individuals weighing up to 100 pounds.

Like all the rodents (gnawers) he has four strong orange-colored teeth or incisors, two in the upper jaw, and two in the lower. Throughout the life of the beavers (and all rodents) these incisors continue to grow, thus compensating for the wear on the cutting edges. The lips are so constructed that they can close behind the incisor teeth, permitting the beaver to gnaw under water.

The eyes of the beaver are small and his sight is apparently not very good. Some authorities claim that he can see very well under water. His hearing is keen in spite of his small ears. When he dives, a valve closes to keep out the water. At the same time, a similar valve closes the nostrils.

The eyes of the beaver are small and his sight is apparently not very good.

Tail is Characteristic Mark

The fore feet are armed with strong claws which are used in digging, combing the fur, and handling the sticks, stones, and mud used for construction work. The manual dexterity developed in the use of the fore feet is remarkable. They are scarcely used in swimming.

The hind feet are completely webbed between five long toes. They are designed for use in the water rather than on land. Consequently, the beaver is awkward and slow when out of the water. The second claw of the hind feet is double. This double claw is used in the combing of the fur, the claws being drawn through hair so as to remove anything clinging to it.

The tail is the characteristic mark of the beaver, by which he differs from all other mammals. It is trowel-shaped, flat, and covered with leather "scales" between which a few coarse hairs may be found. The base is covered with fur. The bare part is about ten inches long.

The uses of the tail are many, but it is not used as a trowel, nor is it used to carry materials. In swimming, it is used both as a rudder and as a powerful propeller. Its function as a rudder is brought into full play when towing branches in the water when it is used to balance the pull on the opposite side.

When cutting trees, the beaver uses his tail as a prop, and as a platform on which to sit, but perhaps its most unique use is as a signaling device. The beaver can slip under the water when diving with scarcely a ripple, but if he is startled he will bring his tail down upon the surface of the water with a resounding thwack and a great splash, thereby warning all other beavers and disappearing himself before the splash has subsided.

The beaver yields a peculiar product called castoreum, which is obtained from musk sacs or "castors." This oily, heavily scented substance was formerly used in medicine. It is now used in the manufacture of certain perfumes. Its chief use is in the baiting of traps. The beaver and many other animals are strongly attracted by its odor.

Once a year, in late spring, from two to six young are born. Occasionally eight are born, but the normal number is four. At birth, they weigh about a pound each.

The "kits" are able to swim at once but are unable to dive for some time as the large amount of air trapped in the fur makes them too buoyant.

Once a year, in late spring, from two to six young are born.

BEAVER

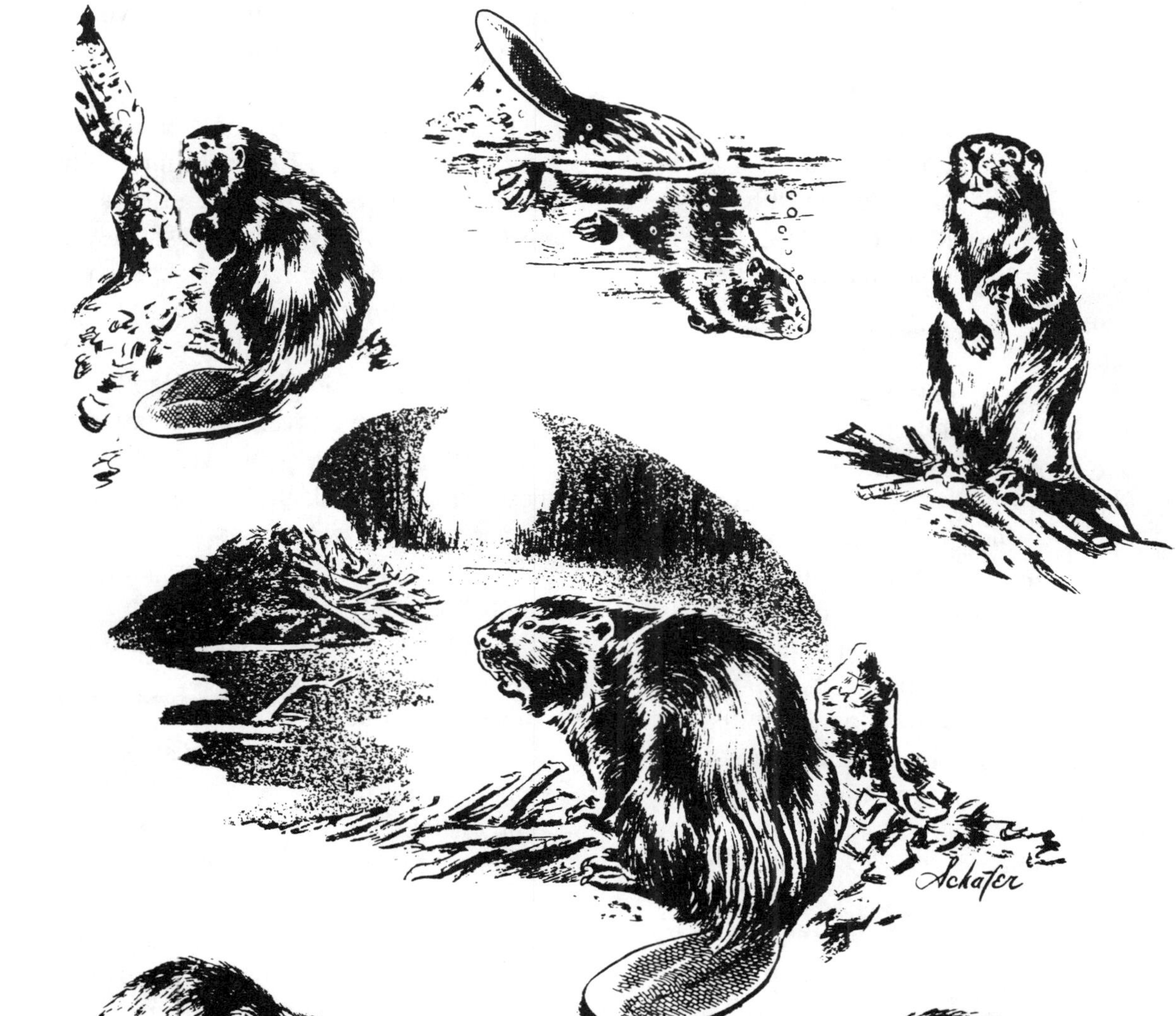

They remain with the family for two winters, after which they wander away to establish homes of their own.

The fur of the beaver consists of very fine, soft, waterproof under-fur which is protected by long, coarse outer hairs.

The fur of the beaver consists of very fine, soft, waterproof under-fur which is protected by long, coarse outer hairs.

The under-fur is so compact that the air contained in it is unable to break the surface tension and escape.

Beavers will commonly spend hours combing their fur, spreading oil over the outer hairs much as certain birds oil their feathers. The oil is obtained from oil sacs. The entrapped air and oil combine to keep water away from the skin. If the beaver is submerged for a long time, water will penetrate part way into the fur. The color varies from tawny yellow through red brown to black.

Beavers Are Vegetarians

Beavers are colonial animals, that is, they live in family groups called colonies, and are characterized by the presence of houses or lodges in which they live, and usually by a dam or series of dams which they construct to facilitate getting food and to provide safety against enemies.

Both lodge and dam are too well-known to need description here. A typical beaver colony consists of an individual family, including the two adult parents, the yearlings born the previous year, and the kits of the current year. The number of beavers in a colony actually varies from one to 12 animals.

The number and size of beaver dams are no indications of the number of animals present, since a single beaver may construct a series of dams under certain conditions, while a colony of beavers on a large river or lake may build no dams at all.

Beavers live entirely on a vegetarian diet, eating a little of everything available in the way of roots, twigs, and bark, but in the Great Lakes region, at least, they really prefer the twigs and bark of aspen (poplar) and alder to anything else.

Their tree cutting ability is well known, and it has been found that under Michigan conditions, each beaver cuts an average of from 200 to 300 trees per year. Many of these trees are sunk underwater near the beaver lodge as winter food when ice covers the surface and beavers cannot forage for food.

Beavers are not the sagacious foresters they are popularly considered to be and frequently fell their trees into one another, thereby wasting a considerable proportion of their work. Some beavers have been killed, found beneath the tree they cut down.

Beaver numbers appear to have increased in recent years as they have learned to live in close proximity to man.

Beaver numbers appear to have increased in recent years as they have learned to live in close proximity to man. In some areas, their dams cause the flooding of roadways.

Beaver

Castor canadensis

Size:	25 to 60 pounds
Range:	Throughout the Great Lakes region.
Habitat:	The beaver prefers slow-moving streams or lakes with young forests giving them access to alder, aspen, or willows.
Fact:	Families of beavers live together in a lodge. Some beavers, depending upon circumstances and conditions, may not build a dam at all.

Great Lakes Mice
Rodents Looking for Opportunity

There are, in the Great Lakes region, excluding Isle Royale, ten forms of native mice and two introduced, or foreign species. Unfortunately, these two undesirable aliens are the ones most familiar to the public, and have come to represent, or rather misrepresent, mice and rats in general.

The two aliens are the house mouse and Norway or barn rat. It is from these that the popular concept of mice and rats as repulsive little vermin has been built up. These two species have lived in close proximity to man since the dawn of history and have acquired some of man's less pleasing characteristics during this long period.

Both are extremely adaptable as to habitat, eat almost everything, breed rapidly, and are probably the most destructive mammals in existence. They are so familiar as to need no description. They are not native to the Great Lakes region or to the American continent, and are mentioned here only because they are, perhaps, the most abundant mammals in the region.

Both are extremely adaptable as to habitat, eat almost everything, breed rapidly, and are probably the most destructive mammals in existence.

Quite different from these aliens are our native mice. No native rats are found in this region, although there are several species native to the United States.

Woods Mice Seldom Damage Crops

Handsomest of our Great Lakes mice are the deer mice and white-footed mice. There are three forms of these in our region, the prairie deer mouse, the woodland deer mouse, and the white-footed mouse. All have long tails, large eyes and ears, pure white bellies and feet, with gray, fawn, or brown upper parts.

The tail is from one-third to one-half the total length and usually bicolored, white below and brownish above. The species are not easily distinguished unless specimens can be examined at close range. These mice are active, agile, hardy, and have a miscellaneous bill of fare, eating all sorts of seeds, thin-shelled nuts, berries, small fruits, insects, and scraps of flesh and bone.

They are believed to be largely responsible for the disappearance of cast-off deer antlers and small skeletal bones left in the woods. These little mice do not usually congregate in numbers, but may occasionally be found in groups of a dozen or more in winter. They seldom do damage to crops. The gestation period is about 21 days and several litters of from two to six young occur each year.

The most abundant of our native mice are the field mice, or meadow voles as they are frequently called. There are four species of these little fellows, each differing in some respects in appearance and in habitat. All are small, about the size of a house mouse, although much heavier built, and with longer hair.

The most abundant of our native mice are the field mice, or meadow voles as they are frequently called.

The red-backed vole is the most striking in coloration, having a broad chestnut band down the middle of the back from forehead to rump, contrasting with the gray body color. The red-backed vole is not abundant and live principally in hardwood forests and conifer swamps.

The pine vole is a small auburn mouse with a very short tail, living in deciduous forests and brushy areas with considerable ground cover of leaves or grass. Pine voles are rarely abundant.

The prairie vole is apparently found only in the extreme southwestern Michigan and in the states of Indiana, Illinois, Wisconsin, and Minnesota. It has tiny ears and eyes. It is similar in general to the common meadow vole, also known as field mouse, which is slightly larger than the voles already described, and far more abundant.

These voles prefer to live in moist, low areas with rank growths of grass. In winter, they may congregate under corn shocks and in other sheltered spots where food is plentiful. Nests are made in grass or in underground burrows, and runways roofed with grass betray the presence of the animals.

The voles breed throughout the year, from one to nine young being born after a gestation period of about 21 days. They are prolific breeders and under favorable circumstances can increase in number to an amazing degree. The remarkable "mouse plagues" of various parts of the world are caused by close relatives of these meadow voles.

Nearly all parts of Europe and Asia, and even some of our western states, have experienced these outbreaks of voles, when literally millions of them overrun large areas, causing as much destruction to cultivated crops and grasslands as though the country had been scourged by fire.

Perhaps the most famous "mouse plague" in America was that in Nevada in 1906-07 when there were estimated to be from 8,000 to 12,000 mice per acre over large areas. So much vegetation was destroyed that fields and even orchards were plowed and re-seeded. Within a year from the time of devastation, most of the mice disappeared and only normal populations remained.

Such mouse plagues have occurred again and again in Europe, and no sure prevention or cure has yet been devised. Fortunately, the Great Lakes region has never experienced one of these catastrophes, although we do have marked cyclic fluctuations in field mouse populations.

The meadow vole is important in this region as a buffer species, since it affords a staple diet for hawks, owls, foxes, weasels, and other predators, which may turn with increased energy to game or poultry when the buffer species are

The meadow vole is important in this region as a buffer species.

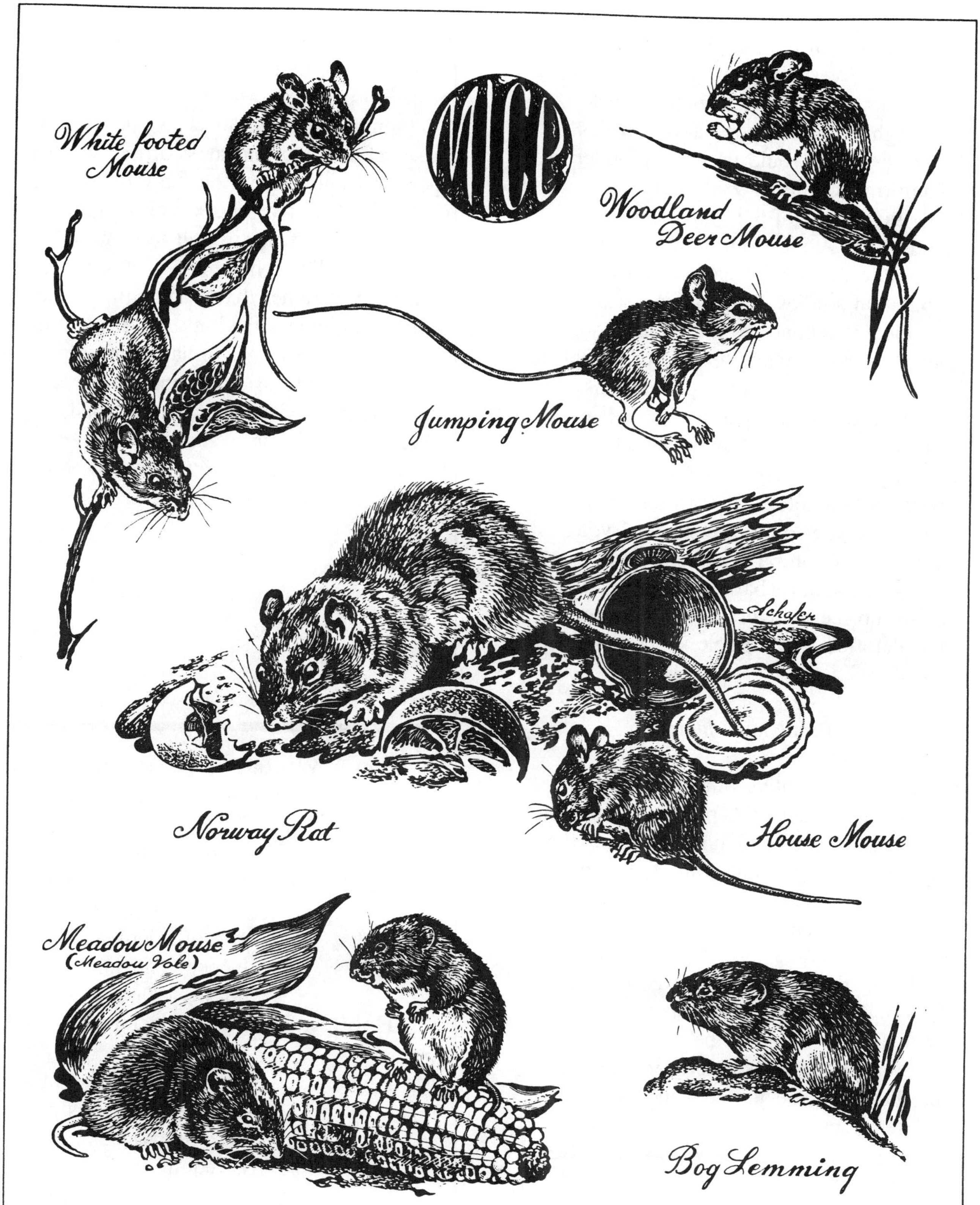
Mice
White footed Mouse
Woodland Deer Mouse
Jumping Mouse
Schafer
Norway Rat
House Mouse
Meadow Mouse (Meadow Vole)
Bog Lemming

at a low ebb in their cycle.

Many investigators of game birds and mammals are inclined to believe that thorough studies of population cycles in the little voles would be more productive of information about game populations than are studies of the game species themselves. Aside from their importance and interest as buffer species and for population studies, the voles possess considerable economic importance, since they do some damage to field crops and to orchards in times of high populations.

Much of the damage to orchards imputed to cottontail rabbits is actually done by voles. They may also eat appreciable amounts of corn left in the fields in winter. Proper control of voles is by means of natural predators, and campaigns against hawks, owls, foxes, etc., should not be inaugurated without due consideration of their role in the control of rodents.

Prodigious Jumpers

Last of the native mice of the Great Lakes region, but perhaps most interesting, are the two species of jumping mice, the meadow jumping mouse and the woodland jumping mouse.

They are characterized by the long, bicolored, scantily-haired tail; the large hind feet; the stiff hairs on the back; and the kangaroo-like method of locomotion. As their names imply, the meadow jumping mouse lives chiefly in open areas and the woodland jumping mouse in forested tracts.

Both species hibernate in winter, and are less prolific than are most of the mice and voles, usually producing only one or two litters of four or five young per year, after a gestation period of about 29 days.

Both species hibernate in winter.

Jumping mice climb vines and bushes in search of food, but most of their time is spent in leaping about on the ground. They can easily leap five or six feet, and their agility makes them difficult to capture. They are inclined, however, to rely upon concealment rather than upon agility, and remain motionless for long periods of time.

They are nocturnal in habit, and are seldom seen. Occasionally they are seen in the headlights of a car on a rural road, when they flash for an instant as they leap lightly off the roadway into the darkness.

White-Footed Mouse
Peromyscus leucopus

Size:	.5 to 1.1 ounces
Range:	Throughout the Great Lakes region except rare in Michigan's Upper Peninsula and northern Ontario.
Habitat:	Prefers deciduous woodlands.
Fact:	In nature, 98 percent die in a year, thus a high reproductive rate is required.

Woodland Deer Mouse

Peromyscus maniculatus

Size: .5 to 1 ounce

Range: Throughout the Great Lakes region.

Habitat: Prefers a wide variety of habitats, the woodland subspecies prefers deciduous forests.

Fact: The deer mouse and its several subspecies, enjoys one of the largest ranges of any North American mammal. It is found almost throughout the continent.

Jumping Mouse

Size: .4 to 1 ounce

Range: Throughout the Great Lakes region.

Habitat: The meadow jumping mouse (*Zapus hudsonius*) prefers open meadows while the woodland jumping mouse, (*Napaeozaus insignis*), prefers coniferous forests.

Fact: May be seen jumping as high as ten feet, propelled by powerful hind legs.

Meadow Mouse (Meadow Vole)

Microtus ochrogaster

Size: 1.1 to 2.1 ounces

Range: Southwestern Michigan and most of the other Great Lakes states.

Habitat: Prefers weedy areas, ungrazed pastures, etc.

Fact: Voles are an important food source for other animals. Other vole species are found in the Great Lakes region.

Bog Lemming

Synaptomys cooperi

Size: .7 to 1.6 ounces

Range: Throughout the Great Lakes region.

Habitat: The bog lemming is found in a variety of habitats from upland forests to swamps. It is rarely seen, however.

Norway Rat
Rattus norvegicus

Size: 7 to 17 ounces
Range: Throughout the Great Lakes region.
Habitat: The Norway rat thrives in close association with humans, thus it is found in urban and suburban areas. It may move into cultivated fields in the summer.
Fact: This mammal is responsible for more destruction of human food than any other throughout the United States.

House Mouse
Mus musculus

Size: .5 to .8 ounces
Range: Throughout the Great Lakes region.
Habitat: The house mouse occurs in many environments but is most common is buildings associated with humans.
Fact: House mice have some homing ability so capturing them alive and then releasing them takes some consideration.

The Muskrat--
Champion Fur Bearer

If we were to stop the "man on the street" and ask him abruptly "what is the most valuable fur bearing animal?" he would probably think of the regal ermine, the romantic sable, the glamorous beaver, or the sleek otter and mink.

Yet the most valuable fear bearer is beyond a doubt the lowly muskrat, the "beaver's little brother," as the Indians called him, for in North America the muskrat far outdistances all other animals in number and total value of pelts marketed.

Peak Prices in 1919-21

This was not always true, of course, for the pioneer trappers who explored so much of North America were after the larger and more spectacular mammals, already mentioned. Small populations and limited markets demanded the larger skins. Muskrats were of so little importance in the region in the early days that few historians even mentioned them, and the little information available must be obtained from trappers' diaries and letters.

Muskrat fur achieved sudden and sensational commercial importance at the time of World War I, when pelts sold for several dollars each, and reached the peak about 1919 to 1921 when muskrat pelts frequently sold for $5 or $6 each.

Severe restrictions were placed on muskrat trapping in 1925, and trapping was allowed in only two months in the three seasons between 1926 and 1929. The decline in muskrat numbers was attributed largely to over-trapping, but perhaps even more important was the destruction of muskrat habitat by drainage of marshes for farmland, and pollution by industrial wastes.

Since 1929 a one- or two-month, or longer trapping season has been permitted in most of the Great Lakes states.

Pelts are Big Business

Louisiana is the top muskrat state with one to two million pelts produced annually. Other leading states are Michigan, Minnesota, Ohio, Pennsylvania, and Wisconsin. Each produces between one third and three quarters of a million hides every year. Some muskrats are produced in practically every state except Florida and Hawaii.

Muskrat fur used to be sold under various trade names which seem to have more glamour than the simple word "muskrat." Among these names were: plucked beavers, wallaby, velvet coney, Hudson seal, Bisam mink, brook mink, electric seal, loutrine, Red River seal, river mink, river sable, silver muskrat, water mink. Now, laws require that these

Muskrat fur used to be sold under various trade names which seem to have more glamour than the simple word "muskrat."

names be dropped and his real name must be used.

Like his "big brother" the beaver, the muskrat lives in the water, builds a house to live in, and has a flat scaly tail. However, a look at the sketches will show distinct differences in the tails of the muskrat and beaver. The tail of the muskrat is flattened laterally--sideways, and the tail of the beaver is flattened dorso-ventrally--top and bottom. An examination of their houses will show some differences also.

The beaver's house is made of sticks and mud, the muskrat's house is made of grass, cattails, rushes, or other vegetation, with little or no mud. The beaver's house is far more solid and permanent in construction, as well as much larger.

Another curious difference between the muskrat and the beaver is in their dispositions. Both are aquatic animals, very much at home in the water, but slow, clumsy, and at a disadvantage on land. One might naturally expect that they would react in a similar way when out of their watery habitat.

The beaver's house is far more solid and permanent in construction, as well as much larger.

This is not so, however. The big, powerful beaver is very much alarmed when surprised on land, and usually makes a clumsy heading rush for the nearest water. If headed off in this rush, he may sit quietly waiting to see what comes next, or may make a few threatening gestures. Rarely does a beaver actually attack his opponent, and a man can generally pick up even an adult beaver and carry him away without much resistance.

The little muskrat, on the other hand, fights savagely when surprised out of water, and does not wait to be attacked, either. Countless cases are on record of muskrats making unprovoked attacks on people, even on city streets. In such cases, the muskrats rush savagely at their fancied opponents, chattering and biting, and attempting to climb up their legs. This apparently senseless rage on the part of so feeble a creature has given rise to the idea that the animals have rabies, like "mad" dogs, but this is seldom, if ever, true. Perhaps the amazing attacks temporarily disconcert opponents, permitting the muskrats to escape in a sufficient number of cases to give the habit a survival value.

Muskrats never build dams. Beavers are strict vegetarians, while muskrats eat clams, dead fish, and such other animal matter as they can readily secure in addition to their standard diet of cattails, grass, roots, etc. Like beavers, muskrats frequently construct tunnels and dens in stream banks, as well as houses out in the water. Muskrats also construct little platforms or mounds of grasses and roots near their houses or dens which they use as food caches.

Like beavers, muskrats frequently construct tunnels and dens in stream banks, as well as houses out in the water.

Muskrat young average from four to nine per litter and more than one litter may occur each year. In Louisiana, as many as four litters are obtained per year, while in northern states, two or three litters are not unusual.

Enemies of the muskrat include hawks, owls, foxes, mink, dogs, etc., but none of these alone is very important in holding

MUSKRAT

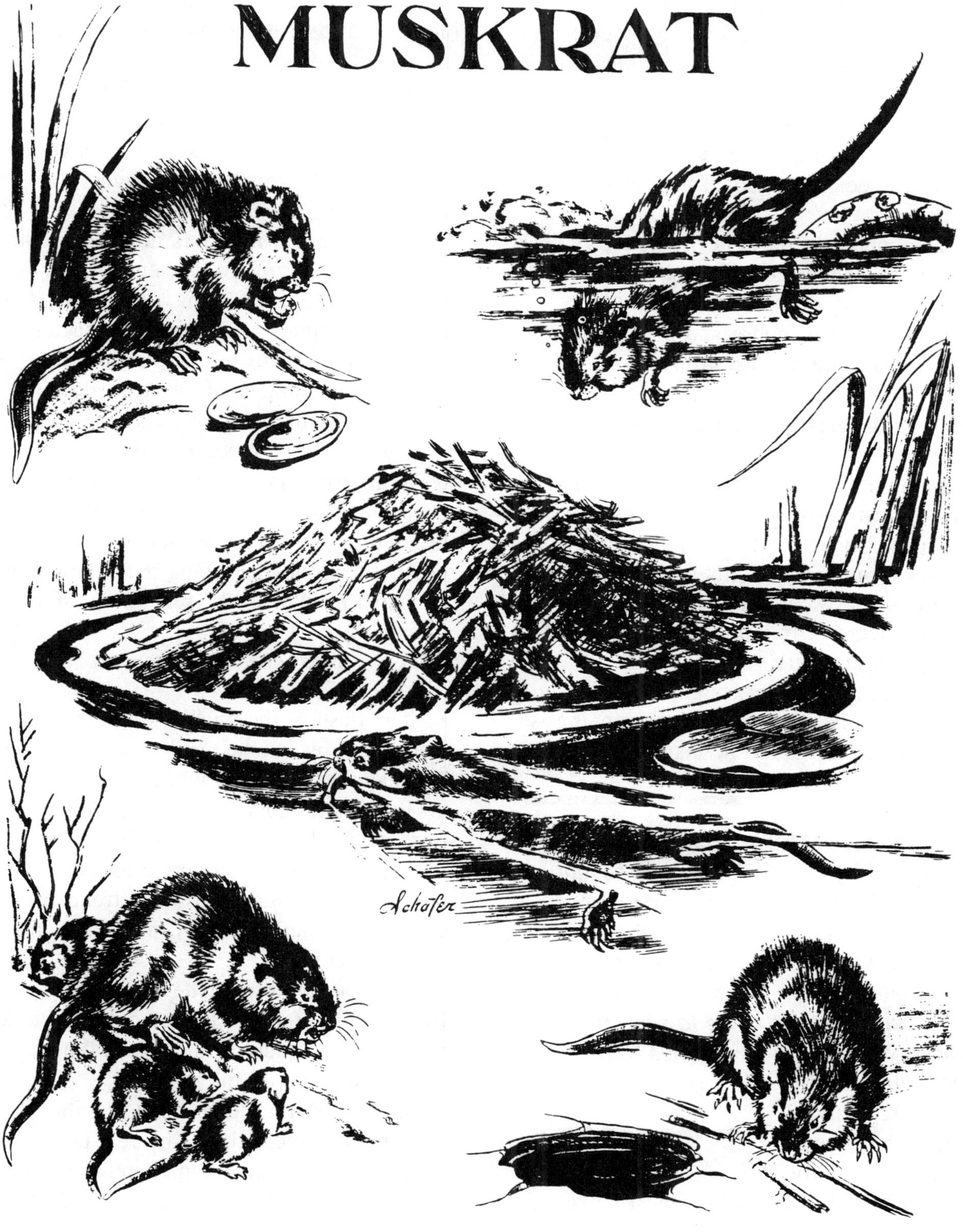

down muskrat populations. One observer noted that he saw a muskrat devoured by a great blue heron--eaten whole in one big gulp!

Even the man with a trap probably takes only part of the annual crop, or surplus, under the seasonal regulations in force.

The annual increase in muskrats is tremendous under normal natural conditions and muskrats frequently "eat themselves out of house and home" if allowed to multiply unrestricted.

Can Be Too Many Muskrats

Many a productive muskrat marsh has been almost destroyed by too many muskrats. Under strictly natural conditions, of course, muskrats migrate when the food supply or the water supply runs short, and in the process of migration may be heavily reduced in numbers.

The ideal objective sought in setting up seasonal regulations on muskrat trapping is to allow the surplus to be taken each year, thereby holding the population to a level which can be maintained by the available food supply.

The ideal objective sought in setting up seasonal regulations on muskrat trapping is to allow the surplus to be taken each year.

Since weather conditions vary unpredictably from year to year, it is impossible to change regulations to meet each year's conditions exactly, and compromise regulations must be set up to take care of the situation.

The muskrat seasons in the zones of each Great Lakes state are set as late as possible to assure getting the best quality fur, yet early enough so that trappers have a fair chance of harvesting most of the muskrats in open water, or at least before trapping conditions get too difficult. The length of season is timed to prevent overtrapping, while allowing the maximum safe harvest of good quality, high value fur.

Spring-caught muskrats might command a small price premium, because the fur is a little more prime in spring than in fall, but a spring trapping season is unsatisfactory for the Great Lakes region because a considerable number of muskrats do not survive the winter here. The spring-caught crop would be so much less than the fall crop that trappers would lose money nearly every year. In addition, much food would be used up during the winter by the larger populations, thus hastening the destruction of marsh habitat for the remaining animals.

Was Once Sold For Meat

The flesh of the muskrat has always been eaten by Indians, and to a considerable extent by white men as well.

In the fall and winter it is not unpalatable, but in the spring it is said to be too musky to be attractive to most tastes. Muskrat meat was once frequently sold in city markets under the trade name "marsh rabbit."

But for the unfortunate stigma conveyed by the word "rat," its flesh would probably have taken its place with various other American game on the table.

It is interesting to speculate on the outcome had the little fur bearers been called by their Indian name "musquash" instead of the Anglicized term "muskrat."

Muskrat
Ondatra zibethicus

Size:	2 to 3.5 pounds
Range:	Throughout the Great Lakes region, in fact, throughout much of North America.
Habitat:	The muskrat is semi-aquatic and prefers lakes, ponds, marshes, and slow moving streams. It is found even in areas where there is much human population.
Fact:	The muskrat mostly eats within 50 feet of its home and rarely goes beyond 500 feet. It is active throughout the day.

The Porcupine--
Prickly Woodland Fool

The North American porcupine is also called quill-pig, prickle-cub, porky hog, and quiller. These terms are of American origin and are in use in various parts of the continent. The term "hedgehog" should not be used, since the true hedgehogs are small, Old World creatures akin to moles and shrews, and are in no way related to our porcupines.

No detailed description of a porcupine seems necessary, as everyone is familiar with the chunky body and formidable spiny armor of the animal. Neither should it be necessary to deny once more the story that porcupines "shoot their quills."

Porcupine quills are rather remarkable things, but they are attached to the skin, and there is no mechanism by means of which they can be hurled like a javelin.

Quills are about one inch long on the head, and four inches long on the back. They are absent from the muzzle, the underparts, and the legs. Each quill is sharp and smooth at the tip, but finely barbed for some distance below the tip. These quills can be erected by voluntary muscles under the skin, and are most formidable weapons of defense. It is estimated that a porcupine is equipped with about 30,000 individual quills.

Porcupine Backs Into Battle

While the quills on the back of the porcupine are purely defensive weapons since an attacker must actually push against them to be hurt, those on the tail are offensive as well. The tail quills are loosely set in the skin, and when the tail is lashed against an enemy, the quills attach themselves very readily to the intruder.

Then the barbs begin their function, and each quill tends to work its way into the flesh. Not only does this cause festering and pain, but if the quills enter the body cavities, they may cause death as well.

The wolverine, for example, is known to commit involuntary suicide by attacking the porcupine regardless of the quills, which penetrate its intestines and cause death.

The smaller cousin of the wolverine, the fisher, seems immune to the quills, and frequently feasts on porcupines without serious injury.

The fisher, seems immune to the quills, and frequently feasts on porcupines without serious injury.

The possession of this tail weapon leads to a ridiculous appearing, but none the less effective, maneuver on the part of the porcupine, for he literally backs into battle, swinging his tail in advance like a medieval mace.

In addition to their great defensive value to the animal, porcupine quills provided the North American Indians with one of their distinctive native arts, ornamentation by quills. This art seems to have been unknown in Europe, but practiced pretty nearly all over North America.

The quills were drawn into, or sewed in patterns upon, garments, moccasins, robes, pouches, quivers, etc.; and were combined with feathers and beads in the ornamentation of war bonnets, pipes, and other ceremonial objects. Quills were bent and woven into baskets, mats, canoes, and small articles, while short ones were strung like beads for fringes. Frequently they were dyed with vegetable juices since their own colors were easily faded or soaked out.

Hemlock is Preferred Food

In summer, porcupines eat all sorts of leafy vegetation, and are particularly fond of lily roots and such other aquatic vegetation as can be found along the edges of lakes and streams.

In winter, the food consists largely of the bark and twigs of hemlock, aspen, jack pine, elm, basswood, etc., although hemlock is perhaps preferred to all else.

Porcupines do not like to exert themselves unduly, and usually live in a single tree until they have pretty nearly used up all available food. Hemlocks are sometimes denuded of every leaf and twig in this way.

Porcupines do not like to exert themselves unduly.

Porcupines are also notorious for their "salt tooth." They are so eager for salt that they will gnaw anything with an iota of briny flavor. Many persons have found their forest cabins practically ruined by these animals. After gnawing through a door, they tackle each and every wooden article within, from meat block to soup ladle.

All cooking utensils are gnawed, as are all wooden articles which have been handled by people. The trace of salt left by sweaty hands is believed to be the cause of this havoc. Incidentally, this damage to cabins is probably the cause of more enmity against porcupines than anything else, even the real damage sometimes done to forest trees.

The young, usually one or two, are born in late winter or early spring. They are remarkably large, which points toward a long gestation period. A porcupine at birth weighs more than a pound, and is nearly a foot long, including the tail. It is covered with long black hair, and the quills are present, but soft at the time of birth.

It is interesting to note that a porcupine weighing ten pounds produces a couple of young weighing over a pound each, while a black bear weighing 200 pounds produces a couple of young weighing about half a pound each.

Home Range is Limited

The porcupine nest may be in a hollow tree or log, a cave or hole under a rock, or in a hole under the roots of a tree or stump.

Porcupines utter a wide variety of sounds, none of them particularly agreeable. They sniff, grunt, squeak, whine, mew, chatter, and on occasion even cry much like a child.

The home range of a porcupine is apparently very limited, perhaps more limited than that of any other North American mammal of its size. Two or three suitable trees may suffice a porcupine for an entire winter, and presumably their summer wanderings are also on a small scale.

In pioneer days, a sort of unwritten law

PORCUPINE

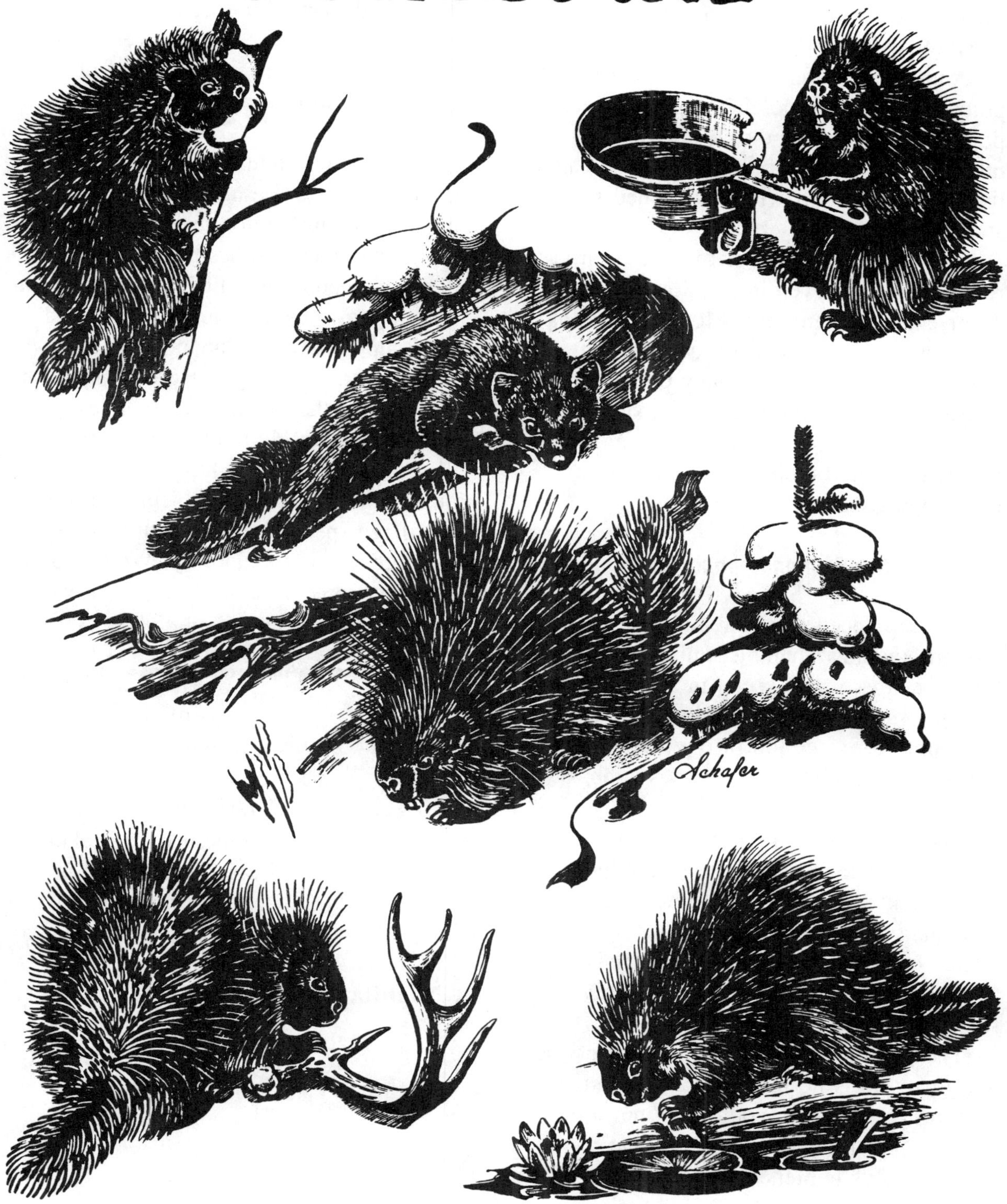

protected porcupines, since a man lost in the woods, without a gun, could at least stave off starvation by killing one of these creatures.

Authorities differ as to the tastiness of porcupine meat, some claiming that young porcupine is very good indeed, while others insist that it is something to be eaten only as a last resort when threatened with starvation.

Porcupines seem never to have been really abundant, even in primitive times. Their enemies were few before the coming of the white man, the wolf, coyote, and fisher probably being the only ones of any consequence. Probably their own slowness and stupidity, together with their small litters, prevented them from building up high populations.

Little Economic Importance

The top speed of a porcupine on the ground is a slow shamble, but even this is fast compared to his speed in a tree. About the only mammal which a porcupine could challenge for a tree top race would be a South American sloth, the very symbol of slowness.

The stupidity of the porcupine is proverbial. The animal will waddle into any sort of danger, and will return again and again to the spot where it has been kicked or beaten. Either its stupidity is colossal, or its memory is unbelievably short.

The porcupine's economic importance is not great. He is no longer looked upon as a food reserve for lost woodsmen, nor are his quills of much value as art material.

He annoys hunters when their dogs come howling out of the woods looking like animated pin cushions after a rash encounter with a "porky."

He kills some valuable timber, and he creates chaos in an empty cabin. Yet, on the whole, he is just a grumpy old backwoodsman who doesn't care how the world goes and who has an aversion to company. He is always an object of interest to tourists, particularly to the children.

Perhaps we should contemplate him thoughtfully, for he has attained some objectives which intrigue a good share of the human race. He has developed a defense mechanism which frees him from fear of most enemies; and he utilizes a food supply which is abundant, never failing, and easy to get. He need not fear famine, weather, or natural enemies. Competition in his field is negligible.

In other words, he has reached a high degree of "social security." In return he has sacrificed speed, agility, beauty, strength, intelligence, and amiability. We can only speculate as to whether it has been worth while.

Porcupine
Erethizon dorsatum

Size:	10-31 pounds
Range:	Northern Great Lakes Region, not found in southern portions of Michigan, Wisconsin, or Minnesota.
Habitat:	Prefers forested areas, hemlock and pine are especially favored. Not found in farmland areas.
Fact:	The porcupine "dances" on its hindlegs during courtship.

Snowshoe Hare--
Turncoat of the Snow Lands

Perhaps a good way to begin an article about this mammal is to follow police procedure in publishing the description of a "wanted" criminal, giving first the correct legal name of the man, followed by his various aliases. Thus, we would describe our mammal like this:

Lepus americanus; alias snowshoe hare, snowshoe rabbit, bush rabbit, northern jack rabbit. In the Great Lakes region, his principal aliases are snowshoe rabbit, snowshoe hare, varying hare, and northern jack rabbit.

To carry the criminal analogy still further, the animal also operates under two disguises--a brown summer coat and a white winter coat. The summer coat is reddish brown above, more or less peppered with black tips to the hairs, lighter along the legs, and white underneath. The upper part of the tail is dark gray, the under part white. The ears are tipped with black behind, and bordered with white in front.

The winter coat is pure white with tinges of brown underneath, but with the black ear tips unchanged.

The winter coat is pure white with tinges of brown underneath, but with the black ear tips unchanged.

From this description, it is easy to see where the names varying hare, white hare, and snow rabbit originate. The "snowshoe" term comes from the fact that the feet are very large for the size of the animal, with broad palms, widespread toes and thick hair, enabling them to scamper freely over the surface of the snow.

The peculiarity permits them to outrun or outdodge such enemies as foxes, coyotes, and lynxes in winter when other hares are easily caught as they flounder in the deep snow.

Color Change Due To Moult

Many people believe that the fur of the snowshoe actually changes color with the season. This is not correct. The change seems to be due, not to a change of hair color, but to a moult; the brown coat being shed and a white coat grown in autumn, and the reverse in spring.

Much argument has taken place as to the protective value of the change from brown to white and the reverse. It is obvious that, in general, the snowshoe is less conspicuous in his white coat during the winter and his brown coat during the summer, than if he wore one or the other at all seasons.

However, the change in color by no means corresponds precisely with the spring and fall snows and thaws, and there are frequently periods when the brown coats are conspicuous against a snow background, and when the white coats are startlingly conspicuous against the dull brown background of the snowless weeds or swamps.

In addition to his seasonal color

changes and his winter snowshoe equipment, this hare is also famous for his population cycles. The snowshoe population in almost any area is subject to marked variations from great abundance to extreme scarcity. These variations seem to occur more or less regularly, hence the term "cyclic" used in describing them.

Volumes have been written describing cycles and attempting to explain their cause or causes. In Canada, the Hudson's Bay Company has kept careful records for more than a hundred years, and these records show that during all that time, snowshoe rabbits have undergone these cycles of abundance and scarcity.

While the Hudson's Bay Company has not been vitally interested in the variations in hare populations directly, they have been vitally interested in the populations of such animals as the fox, lynx, fisher, marten, and skunk, which furnish the furs on which the company depends for its trade with the natives. The number of these fur-bearing animals depends upon the number of snowshoe hares, and the cycle of abundance of the fur bearers rises and falls with that of the hares, but somewhat later.

Still more important, the Indian population is almost equally dependent in turn on the hare and fur bearer cycles, and the periods when these animals are scarce are periods of hardship and even starvation for the Indians.

The cycle of abundance of the fur bearers rises and falls with that of the hares, but somewhat later.

Fortunately, the highs and lows of the cycles do not occur precisely together in all parts of the country, so the Indians of one area may be getting along fairly well while those some distance away are in desperate circumstances.

Numbers Vary In Cycles

The course of events during a snowshoe hare cycle seems to run like this: the population apparently increases slowly, with minor ups and downs, for several years; then for a year or two there is a tremendous increase, until there are snowshoes everywhere. They literally swarm, and the total population reaches a fabulous figure.

Ernest Thompson Seton, the famous naturalist, observed one of the periods of top cyclic abundance in Manitoba in 1882, and estimated that there were then over 100 million snowshoes in that province alone. Farmers and ranchers were aghast, and feared disaster to crops and grass.

Yet within a year, the snowshoe population dropped to such a point that it was actually difficult to find a living animal in that same area. While this was, perhaps, an extreme cyclic period, much the same thing occurs periodically throughout the snowshoe's range.

The northern Great Lakes region experiences this ebb and flow of snowshoe numbers, and the amount of hunting or the severity of the winter seem to have no effect on the phenomenon. The cycle seems to have been going on before the dawn of recorded history, and will probably continue far into the future, perhaps long after man has eliminated himself with some of his cosmic contraptions.

The cause of the catastrophic drop from incredible abundance to a scattered remnant seems to be an epidemic which can only develop and spread when animals

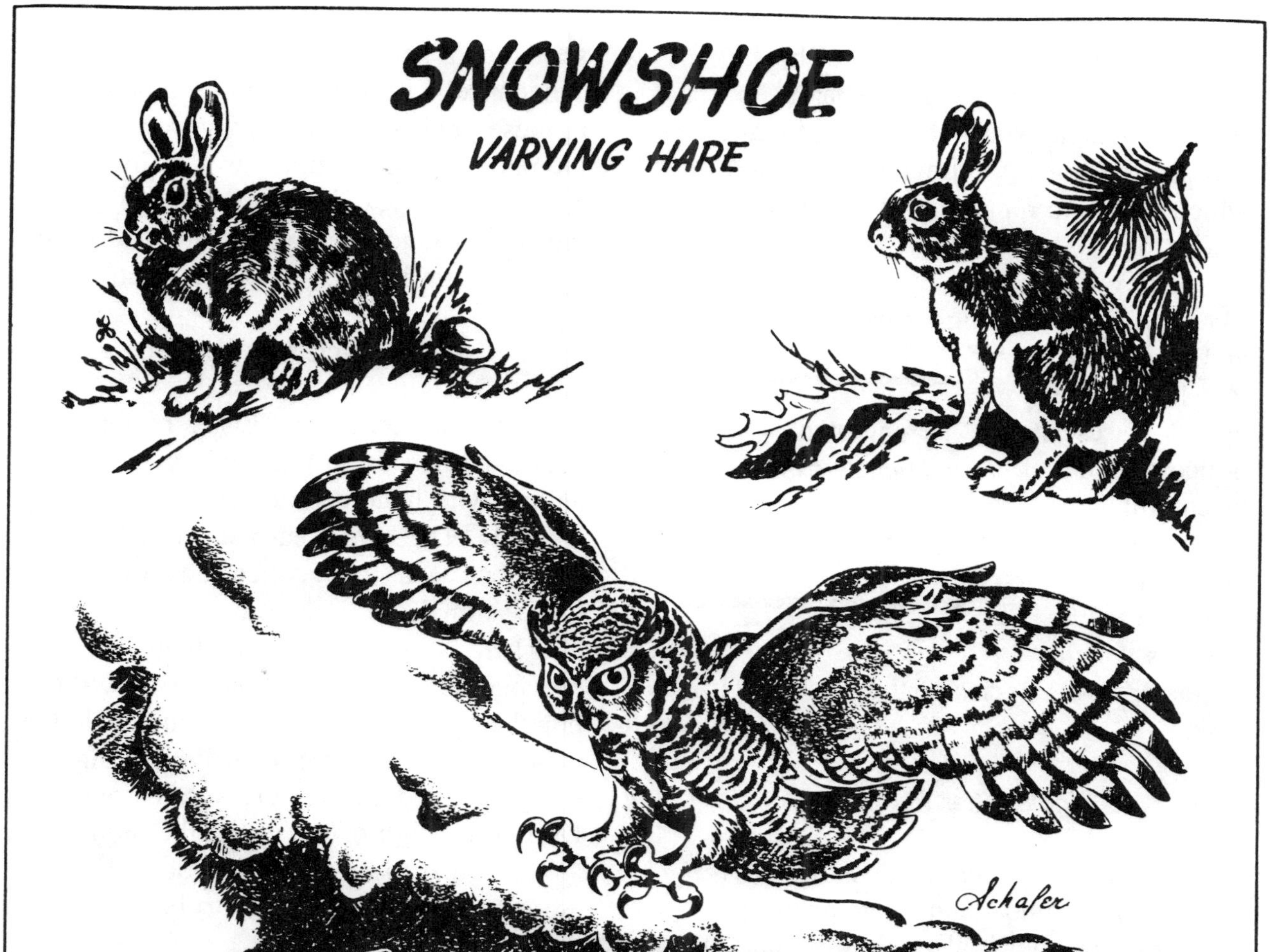
SNOWSHOE
VARYING HARE
Schafer

are crowded at peak abundance. The resurgence is partly due to the rapid recovery which usually follows epidemics, and probably also to climatic influences which speed up reproduction in certain years.

Many other animals exhibit cyclic fluctuations. It is thought that most birds and mammals are to a lesser extent cyclic, but escape notice due to lack of careful observation and lack of the spectacular features which characterize the cycles of the snowshoe hare.

Many other animals exhibit cyclic fluctuations.

Single Litter Per Year

The principal food of the snowshoe is the succulent shoots and twigs of many northern trees, but it also takes the bark of poplar, willow, birch, and others in winter. Contrary to the general habits of the hares and rabbits, snowshoes seem to relish a little meat in their diet, and often get into traps baited with meat for fur bearing animals.

Snowshoes are less prolific than most of their relatives, usually producing but a single litter per year, with an average of about three or four per litter. During the period of rapid cyclic increase, however, as many as six to eight young may be produced per litter.

While its flesh is not so highly esteemed as that of its cousin, the cottontail, it is good to eat, and the animals are one of the staples in the diet of many northern residents. They are also, as already pointed out, the chief reliance of northern fur bearing animals, and of the snowy owl, and a decrease in snowshoe abundance is soon followed by a decrease in these predators. The snowy owls may migrate south, and appear well below their customary range. The mammalian predators cannot readily migrate, and death by starvation is likely to be their fate.

Little Affected by Hunting

In the northern Great Lakes region, the snowshoe hare is an important game animal with hundreds of thousands taken annually. The long open season makes the snowshoe legal game when most other game animals are protected.

There is no evidence that hunting pressure has much effect on our snowshoe population. During the low of the cycle the animals are too scarce to make hunting enjoyable, and hunting pressure is low. During the high of the cycle, the numbers are too great to be seriously affected by any hunting pressure likely to be experienced.

Snowshoe Hare
Lepus americanus

Size:	3 to 5 pounds
Range:	Northern Great Lakes region.
Habitat:	Coniferous or mixed forests, particularly low-lying forests and cedar swamps.
Fact:	The snowshoe hare is not a rodent.

Cottontail Rabbit--
Big Game of the Small Boy

The cottontail rabbit is not only the big game of the small boy, it is also the leading game animal of many Great Lakes states.

The ringnecked pheasant may attract more attention, and draw a bigger crowd for its October debut, but the cottontail has a much longer hunting season and many more cottontails are killed annually. Also, the cottontail occupies a considerable area of the region and the cottontail rabbit is most abundant in areas where the pheasant is comparatively scarce.

The hares and rabbits form a family, the *Leporidae*, scattered widely over the earth, but being most numerous in northern regions where the animals have always been an important food resource for man and beast.

All members of the family are much alike in the long, haunched hind legs which give great leaping and dodging power; tall erectile ears; divided upper lip; and grizzled brown coat, with variations of white and black.

Seldom Seeks Winter Shelter

The term "rabbit" has almost entirely replaced "hare" in America, because the common cottontail of the Atlantic coast, one of the animals first seen by the early settler, looked more like the rabbit they had known in Europe than like their bigger European hares. Also, they ignored the difference in habits as they did so many other facts in their careless naming of the New World animals after those of Europe.

It must be remembered that the Pilgrims, Puritans, and Cavaliers came mostly from cities, and knew little about rural things, to which ignorance they owed many of their hardships and misfortunes in their new home. Hence, the small animal of the eastern and midwestern United States became the "cottontail rabbit," the varying hare of northern regions became the "snowshoe rabbit," and the big-eared hare of the west became the "jack rabbit."

Actually, the typical rabbits are colonial dwellers, living in crowded diggings called "warrens," which are labyrinths of connecting burrows. The young are born in these warrens.

The hares do not dwell in warrens, and the young are born in the open in small depressions called "forms." Only in severe winter weather does our cottontail occasionally enter a woodchuck hole for shelter from the storm, or to escape enemies, while the snowshoe hare and western jack rabbit probably never enter burrows.

New-born Rabbits Safely Hidden

The gestation paired of the cottontail averages 30 days but the time may vary between 25 and 35 days. The first litter is usually born early in April although young are occasionally found even earlier. Three or four litters per year seem to be common in the southern parts of the Great Lakes region.

The female, before the young are born, digs a bowl-shaped depression in the ground about four to six inches in depth and four inches in width which she lines with dry grass and then with fur from her own body.

The young cottontails, which are born blind and helpless, are placed in this nest, where they remain for about two weeks. The average litter is about five, but there is considerable variation. The mother is believed to return from time to time during the night and occasionally during the day to lie over the nest, allowing the young to nurse without leaving their snug haven.

If danger threatens, the mother can dash away, while the nest remains securely hidden. It is difficult to discover a rabbit nest until the young have left it, so well is it concealed. Systematic search often proves fruitless, and nests are usually discovered by chance. The well-concealed nest undoubtedly protects the young from many keen-eyed predators.

The well-concealed nest undoubtedly protects the young from many keen-eyed predators.

Full Bag of Tricks

Cottontails are not as defenseless as is generally believed, and have been observed to defend themselves from cats by leaping over the cat's back, upsetting the cat with blows from the hind legs enroute. The big Belgian hares so common in captivity are reported to defend themselves successfully from dogs in the same way.

Of course, the principal defense of the rabbits and hares is their speed and ability to dodge. They have astonishing skill in halting, doubling, and changing their course, by which means they get a fresh start before their clumsier pursuers can see what has happened and change their own course to correspond.

Along with this go extreme timidity and watchfulness, in which the big ears serve a most useful purpose, rising at the slightest sound, but dropping out of the way as the animal makes off in a series of bounds.

Knowing these tricks, most predators resort to counter strategy, a stealthy approach and quick rush; although a few, like the dog and weasel, may follow the track with stubborn persistence, hoping to overtake and corner their prey eventually.

High Reproductive Rate

However, the characteristic which enables the cottontail to maintain itself in the face of its many enemies, including that most implacable of all, man, is its fecundity. The reproductive ability of the rabbit is traditional, and it has been frequently demonstrated, on paper, that a pair of rabbits, breeding unhindered, could fill a continent with their kind in a few years.

We all realize that in real life the world is not inundated with rabbits, mice, flies, guinea pigs, oysters, or any of the other creatures whose reproductive ability is so fantastic on paper, yet we frequently fail to grasp the implications of this "balance of nature," which holds each species in check.

The cottontail feeds on a great many kinds of plants, wild and cultivated alike. Cottontails eat bark, twigs, buds, fruit, grains, or stems. One might think that food would be no problem to animals with so wide a menu, but this is not a safe assumption. For example, in winter when snow covers grasses and other low growing vegetation, a cottontail may have a hard

COTTONTAIL RABBIT

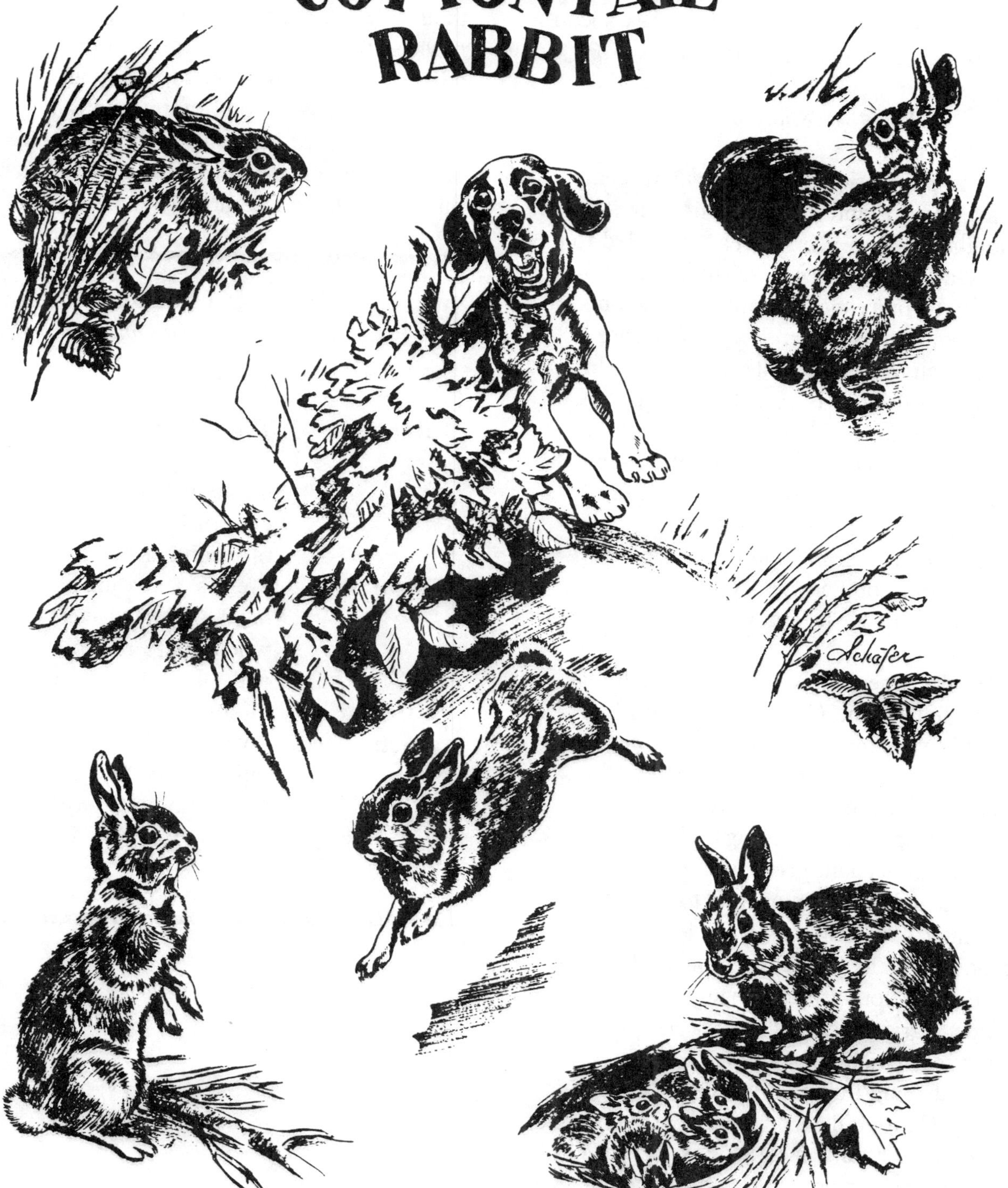

time getting enough food to carry it through, and its danger from predatory enemies is much increased if it must spend additional time searching for food.

Likes A Variety of Cover

The popularity of the cottontail as a game animal, and local variations in abundance from year to year, have led to many attempts to increase the number of rabbits to make better hunting. Attempts to raise cottontails in captivity for release have been very discouraging.

The cottontail is essentially a species of the borderlands, neither forest nor plains. It is fond of places overgrown with young conifers, thickly crowded together, or thickets of briers and brambles. It rejoices in abandoned farms, and occupies, by preference, coppices and grassy spots near cultivated areas. It is not contented in deep forests.

For a time following the agricultural settlement of the Great Lakes region, nearly everything done by the farmer was of benefit to the cottontail. Clearing the land, planting patches of crops, brush growing up in the clearings, zigzag rail fences, clover and grass pastures, all proved highly advantageous to cottontails.

Later developments were less beneficial. The rail fence was replaced by wire; woodlots grazed cleanly; swamps burned; grain picked clean; stone piles removed; woodchucks killed. All this seemed to add up to a gloomy outlook for Molly Cottontail.

However, in some sections, contour farming, newer crop rotation methods, mechanical harvesters that leave waste grain, reduced spring burning, elimination of woodlot grazing, all tend to give Molly and Peter Cottontail a better opportunity for raising bigger and better families.

Now if we can persuade farmers to pile brush in big heaps, let woodchucks live in their holes in the woods, gullies, and fence rows, and let some brush grow around the edge of the woodlot, perhaps we can continue to enjoy good rabbit hunting, even in the face of the ever increasing army of hunters who take to the field in pursuit of the big game of the small boy.

Cottontail Rabbit
Sylvilagus floridanus

Size:	2 to 4 pounds.
Range:	Throughout the Great Lakes region except northern Ontario and eastern Upper Peninsula of Michigan.
Habitat:	Prefers a mixture of habitats, but thrives where there are thickets and places to create hiding spots.
Fact:	Average life span in the wild is less than a year but some have lived as long as four years.

The White-Tailed Deer--
Big Business Mammal

Our white-tailed deer, also called Virginia deer, is a member of the family *Cervidae*, or, in everyday terms, the deer family.

Amid all the various technicalities which so often distinguish one family or group of animals from another, it is a comfort to find a family all of whose member species are recognized by a single characteristic. It is enough to say that a deer is an animal which bears antlers.

Antlers are bony projections on the head which are grown and shed periodically. Antlers must not be confused with horns. Horns are also bony projections on the head, but they are hollow, and are not shed and grown anew.

When a horn is broken off, it is gone, and it is not replaced. Cows, sheep, goats, antelopes, and so forth are examples of horned animals. Only the deer grow and shed their bony head ornaments yearly. Many persons seem to accept readily the fact that deer grow new antlers each year, but find it difficult to believe that the mighty palmate antler of the moose, or the magnificent rack of the elk are similarly products of a single summer.

Antlers Are Fighting Weapons

It is has been estimated that it takes about as much energy, although only half as much time, to produce a pair of antlers as to produce a fawn. Of what purpose and value is this elaborate headgear, which costs annually half the time and strength of the animal, only to be cast aside when winter comes?

Apparently, antlers serve their possessors principally for fighting with rival bucks for the possession of does, and their importance disappears with the end of the mating season.

So familiar is the white-tailed deer to Americans that we need no detailed description of his size, or of his grace and speed. We may need reminding that our deer change color with the season, from a reddish or rufous shade in summer to a grayer, rougher looking coat in winter.

In either coat, the under side of the plumelike triangular tail is snow white. When the deer runs this tail is erected, and the white undertail marking waves like a banner, from whence comes the popular name, whitetail.

Deer change color with the season, from a reddish or rufous shade in summer to a grayer, rougher looking coat in winter.

The whitetail is essentially a dweller in a diversified habitat where woods and swamps alternate with open glades and swales. Whitetails are neither creatures of the deep forest nor of the open prairie, and much of their present range in the Great Lakes region was not occupied by them to any considerable extent before the coming of the lumberman with axe and crosscut saw.

Following the great lumbering era of the 1800's, young forest growth came up everywhere in the region, and whitetails increased in numbers correspondingly. Then, extensive fires over much of the north country laid waste the land, and delayed the development of new forests and deer alike. With the establishment of an improved fire fighting organization and motorized equipment, fires were controlled and the deer population again swung sharply upward. Now, forests are becoming so widespread, and the trees so tall and thick, that our deer population may have passed its peak in some areas.

Deer Are Browsing Animals

During the spring, summer, and fall months, whitetails roam freely over the countryside, finding food almost everywhere. At this time, the animals eat herbs, grain, leaves, and succulent material of all sorts. We must keep in mind, however, that deer are not grazing animals like cattle and sheep, but browsing animals.

They do eat some grain but their real "bread and butter" diet consists of twigs and leaves. Now twigs and leaves are very easy to get in summer, and can be readily supplemented with other material also, but in winter, when the snow is deep, deer cannot get around through the open country, but are confined to so-called "yards" in dense woods and swamps.

Here, they must eat what is at hand, and here it is that starvation sometimes faces them. The habitable area available to our Great Lakes whitetails in a winter of deep snow is only about one-fifth that available during other seasons, except in the southern parts of the region.

The situation is roughly comparable to that on a farm where the cattle herd has plenty of pasture for summer, but must be brought into the barnyard to be fed during winter. But whereas cattle can readily be fed hay and grain in the barnyard, deer cannot be handled in this way and other methods of management must be adopted.

The practical approach to this problem, and indeed the one most beneficial to the deer herd and most rewarding to the sportsman, is to take by hunting, every year, the surplus over and above the optimum breeding herd. This leaves a minimum number of deer to be fed by the scarce supply of natural winter food. This rather simple procedure is not well understood by the general public, and has been the subject of much controversy in some areas.

Fawns Should Be Let Alone

The gestation period of the whitetail is approximately seven months, and the young are born principally in May and June. Twins are very common, so that the annual increase may be computed at about a fawn and a half per doe.

The fawns are pretty little spotted fellows, and the spots are visible for several months. Fawns are friendly and unsuspicious for some time after birth, and are often discovered and captured by people at this time, under the mistaken notion that they have been deserted by the mother and are in need of assistance. Every year, the public is warned that it is not only entirely unnecessary to pick up fawns in the woods, but that it is strictly illegal as well. Yet, the practice continues.

Fawns are friendly and unsuspicious for some time after birth.

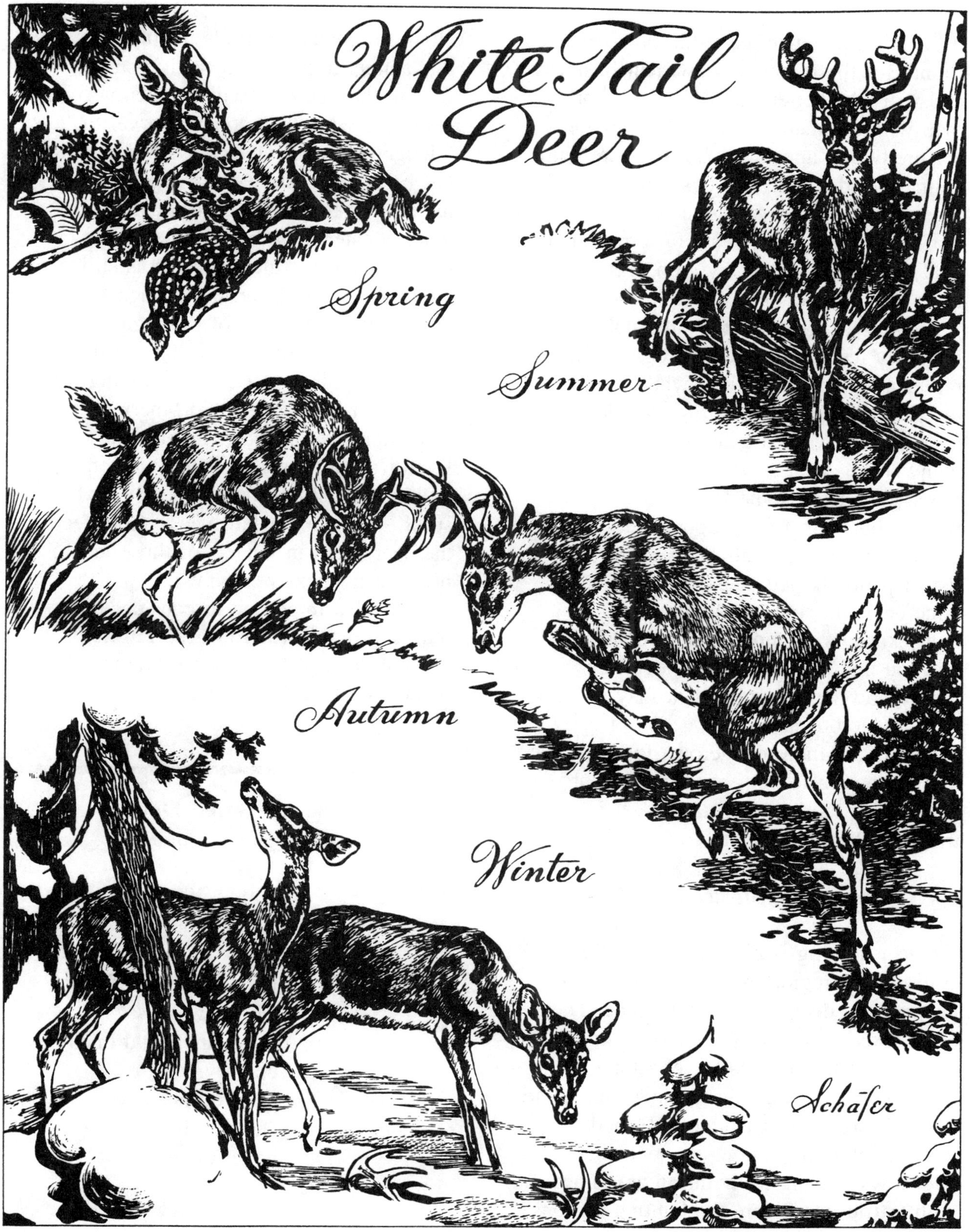
White Tail Deer
Spring
Summer
Autumn
Winter
Schäfer

It is far better to leave the fawns where found, for the mothers know their business and will take better care of their offspring than will a human foster mother. Fawns are pretty and appealing, but they are wild animals, and should be considered as such.

We think of deer as graceful, timid, inoffensive creatures, beautiful ornamental pets to show off and play with. Yet an adult deer, particularly an adult buck, is just about as safe as a pet rattlesnake. Probably less safe, for we recognize the rattler as a potential killer, while we forget the potential deadliness of a buck deer.

Not only women and children, but many strong men as well, have met with tragic ends from some "tame" deer--doe as well as buck--that was supposed to be the gentlest, loveliest creature on earth. The list of people killed or gravely injured by tame deer runs into the hundreds, and many keepers of zoological gardens will tell you that an adult captive deer, no matter how tame or playful it may appear, is as dangerous as a captive lion or grizzly bear. In fact, more dangerous, for everyone knows enough to beware of the lion or bear, while the beautiful tame deer is trusted until it is too late.

Increase Is Greater Than Kill

Deer hunting is big business in the Great Lakes region. More than a million people hunt deer in Michigan alone. They often take home nearly 200,000 deer.

Most of the hunters travel a long distance to their hunting grounds and spend a lot of money on gasoline, oil, food, lodging, clothing, and equipment. Highways leading to the north are jammed with traffic just before the hunting seasons and northern cabins and hotels are crowded beyond their capacities.

Many people who enjoy seeing deer along the roads and trails in summer view this annual deer hunting with dismay, fearing that the deer will be decimated, and deploring what they consider a veritable "slaughter of the innocents." Actually, it has been demonstrated that the annual increase of the Great Lakes deer herd is much greater than the annual kill by hunters, and that the deer herd is still larger than can be carried through severe winters in many parts of the region.

Hunters merely help to harvest the annual surplus of deer, thus utilizing for food animals which would otherwise perish from starvation or other natural causes. Even from a purely aesthetic viewpoint, hunting is justified for the removal of surplus deer in the fall means more feed in the deer yards in winter for those left to produce the next year's fawns.

It is also important to consider that reducing the deer herd in the fall helps prevent damage to crops and the number of potentially fatal car-deer accidents on our highways.

White-Tailed Deer

Odocoileus virginianus

Size:	100 to 300 pounds
Range:	Throughout the Great Lakes region.
Habitat:	Prefer a mix of forests, dense swamps, brushlands, and open country.
Fact:	Deer do not have "horns," instead they have "antlers."

Moose and Elk--
Giants of the Antlered World

Early records show that moose and elk were once present in considerable numbers in the Great Lakes region, although it is difficult to determine their exact range and relative abundance.

This is because the ranges of moose, wapiti (American elk), woodland caribou, and white-tailed deer overlapped in the region and because the names of each species and of deer in general--common and technical in both French and English--were so loosely used.

The European "elk" and the American "moose" are so nearly identical that only an experienced taxonomist (one who is able to classify animals according to their natural relationships) can distinguish between them; hence, the French explorers called our moose the "elan," French term for elk.

Then they saw the big American wapiti, and called that "elan" also. The English explorers were thoroughly confused among the various Indian and French names, so that in reading early American records we can never be quite sure whether an "elk" was a "wapiti" elk, or a moose. Today, however, we clearly distinguish the elk and moose as found in America.

Both Are Great Lakes Mammals

Both moose and elk seem to have become extinct throughout much of the Great Lakes region, following the lumbering era. But both have since been reintroduced, and are found in increasing but limited areas at the present time.

Due to their great size and importance in pioneer days, they should be considered among Great Lakes mammals, despite their relative scarcity or limited range.

The moose is a huge, immensely strong and ungainly animal, blackish brown with pale legs and belly, and with a neck so short that it can graze only by kneeling or straddling. A big bull moose may stand six and a half feet at the withers, which with the neck are clothed in a thick mantle of long, coarse, stiff hair.

The moose is a huge, immensely strong and ungainly animal.

From the throat hangs a long, hairy strip of dewlap skin called a "bell," which in old age draws up into a sort of pouch. The long narrow head ends in an overhanging flexible muzzle, which can be curled around a twig almost like an elephant's trunk.

On this massive head and neck the bull carries a tremendous pair of flattened antlers. Antlers are preserved which have a spread of over six feet, carrying more than thirty points, and measuring 15 inches around the base or burr. Yet these mighty antlers, like the lesser ones of a deer, are shed each winter, and grown entirely anew each summer. An adult bull moose may weigh as much as 1,500 or 1,600 pounds.

The moose is a creature of the forest, particularly of well-watered forests. Rough terrain and thick vegetation seem to trouble the moose little, for he clambers over steep slopes with ease, and crashes through the thickest brush like a tank.

Moose are fond of wading into the water neck deep in summertime, eagerly devouring aquatic vegetation, often going completely under after lily roots. They are splendid swimmers and do not hesitate to cross lakes several miles in width.

Moose "Yard" in Snowy Winters

Moose eat the leaves and twigs of both hardwoods and conifers as available in season. Trees of considerable size are straddled and pushed down so that the foliage may be reached.

In autumn, the bulls, their freshly grown antlers strong and bright, roam the woods in search of mates, bawling out invitations and challenges day and night. The challenges are frequently accepted, and terrific combats between rivals follow.

At this time, they are in prime condition, and are much sought by hunters, since a good pair of moose antlers is considered a prize trophy. Moose may be hunted by stalking, or by "calling" with birch bark horns. A skilled moose caller can duplicate the challenge of a bull moose to perfection, bringing the animal right up to the hunter's rifle. A wounded or cornered bull moose is a dangerous customer, for he charges like a locomotive and is hard to stop.

Moose calves are born in late spring, and are ridiculous creatures with their long awkward legs and long clumsy lips. They are readily tamed and reared in captivity, and have been trained to pull sledges in Canada and Scandinavia.

Like deer, moose "yard" in snow winters. Their yards are merely areas where they feed and keep the snow trampled hard as they browse about. In the course of a long winter these areas are connected with a labyrinth of paths, tramped as hard as human roadways.

While in the yards, the moose are in little danger from predators, for even the timber wolf cannot successfully attack a full-grown moose on even terms. Only when there is a crust on deep snow is the moose in danger, for his feet are too small to support his great weight, and the wolf can run on the crust while the moose flounders helplessly in the deep snow. Hence, moose confine themselves closely to the yards and paths, only venturing into the snow when their yard becomes overbrowsed and a fresh food supply must be reached at once.

Moose confine themselves closely to the yards and paths.

At this time, moose are found in Michigan only in the Upper Peninsula and on Isle Royale National Park in Lake Superior. They are also found in extreme northern Wisconsin and Minnesota and in Ontario.

Moose always retreat before the advance of civilization and there is little likelihood that they will ever again occur in great numbers on the mainland.

Elk Were Once Abundant

The elk, or wapiti, is perhaps the most stately member of the deer family. Not as big as the moose, the elk is far more graceful in appearance, and has always been eagerly sought as a subject for painter and photographer. An adult bull elk may weigh seven hundred pounds and stand

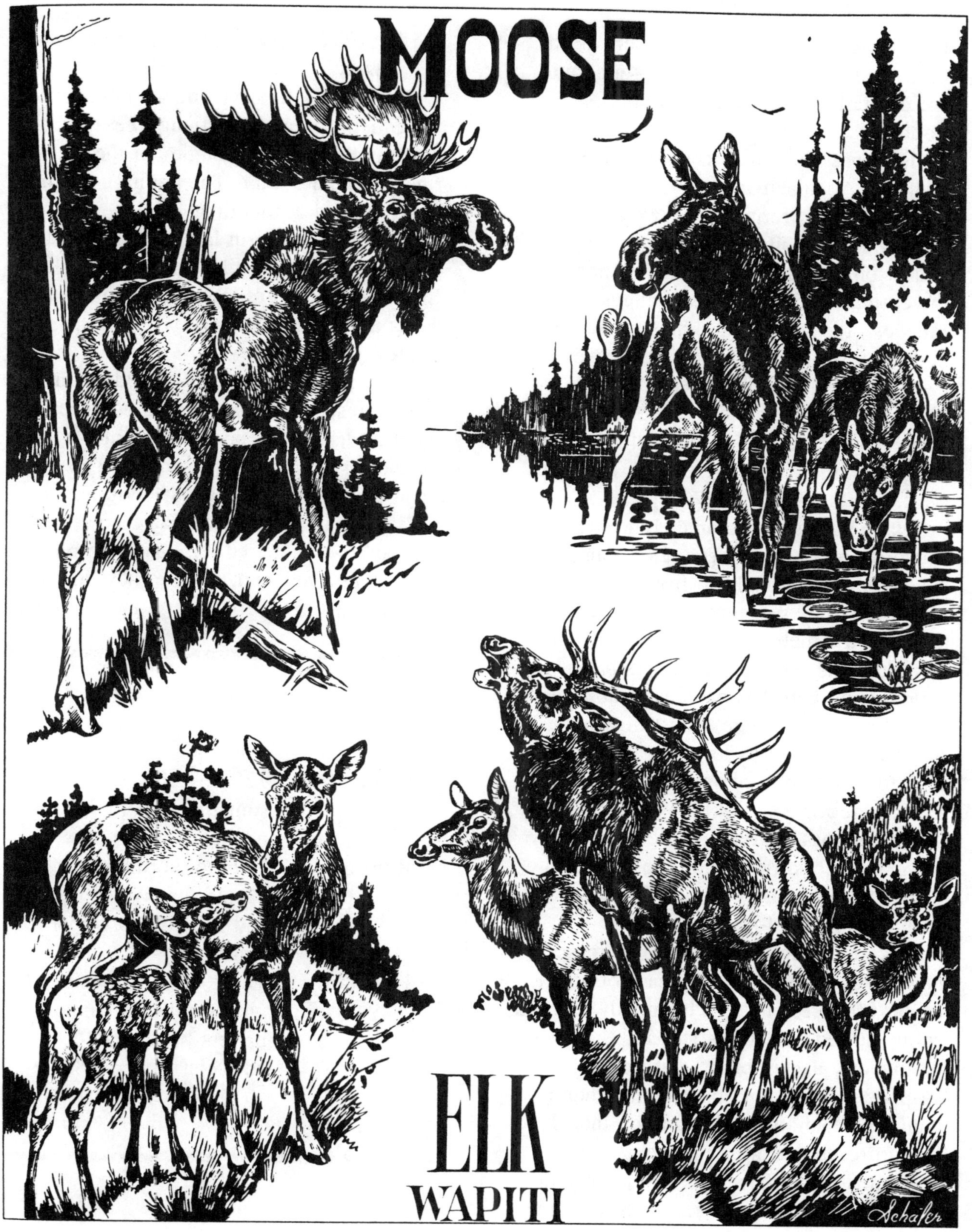
MOOSE
ELK
WAPITI
Schafer

five feet at the withers. Elk antlers are the most symmetrical of the deer group, and are naturally highly prized as hunting trophies.

Elk once abounded in North America from the Appalachians to the coast of Alaska and California. They were less limited as to habitat than were the moose and bison, and seemed equally at home in the eastern forests, the lush valleys of the midwest, the sun-baked plains of Nebraska, and the towering sierras of the far west.

Unfortunately, elk are easy to hunt and kill, and the pioneers destroyed them as they moved west. Long since eliminated in the plains, elk still survive in parts of the west.

Native elk were completely destroyed in much of the Great Lakes region long ago, but have been brought in from the Jackson Hole region of Wyoming, and released from captive herds as well. Most of the introductions resulted in failures but a reproducing herd has become established in the Pigeon River State Forest of Michigan and has expanded its territory. A herd is also found in west-central Ontario near Lake Superior.

Elk enjoy a diversified diet, since they eat grass, moss, lichens, and other small vegetation as well as the leaves, twigs, and bark of hardwood trees.

Like deer and moose, they "yard" in periods of deep snow. The yard of a band of elk often resembles a barnyard, with the snow packed as hard as ice, and the trees, particularly aspen, birch, and willow, stripped of twigs and bark higher than a man can reach. The elk stand on their hind legs to reach the higher branches. Naturally, the younger elk fare poorly in competition with the big fellows, and may starve when deep snow remains for an extended period.

Elk Readily Kept in Captivity

In the fall, the necks of the bulls swell, the antlers spread like young trees, and the defiant challenge, or "bugle" of the elk, rings through the air. The animals are most easily hunted at this time.

Young are born in late spring, and the life history is much like that of other deer. Elk are readily kept in captivity, and small herds are often seen in zoos and on private estates.

Like moose, elk are not fitted to thrive in the presence of civilization, and seem fated to disappear except in remote regions or under special legal protection. The majestic monarchs of the wilderness, like human kings and emperors, are now reduced to a scattered remnant, allowed to survive in a few spots where they do not interfere with modern tempos and methods.

Moose
Alces alces

Size:	725 to 1,100 pounds, sometimes to 1,600 pounds.
Range:	Ontario, northern Minnesota, Wisconsin, and Michigan's Upper Peninsula.
Habitat:	Thick, boreal forests with shrubs, in summer prefers brushland adjacent to wetlands.

Elk
Cervus elaphus

Size:	500 to 1,000 pounds.
Range:	Central northern Michigan and west-central Ontario.
Habitat:	Open meadows or woodlands with access to grasslands.
Fact:	In a zoo, elk may live 20 years. Generally, they live about 10 years in the wild.

Vanished Mammals

Several of the Great Lakes region's most interesting mammal species disappeared with the advent of the white man, although in some cases the disappearance may not have been the result of pioneering activities.

Some of these species have already been mentioned. They are the wolverine, fisher, marten, lynx, and elk. It is true that elk, marten, fisher, and lynx, have been imported and released and that a small number exists in the region at this time. But our native elk, marten, fisher, and lynx are extinct.

In the case of three species, the disappearance was complete, and no reliable reports of their presence have been heard for a century. These are the bison, caribou, and puma.

It may surprise many people to learn that the bison, or buffalo, as it was commonly but erroneously called, once roamed the open areas of the southern Great Lakes region. Nevertheless, it certainly did so, and was reported by many early explorers and pioneers. It was probably never so abundant and conspicuous in this region as it was on the great prairies of the west.

Bison Once Among Most Important

The bison is the largest of American mammals, and was at one time the most important game mammal as well.

Everyone is familiar with the story of the slaughter of the bison on the western prairies by Buffalo Bill and other famous characters of the wild west era in American history. After careful research, Ernest Thompson Seton estimated the population of bison in America in primitive times to have been at least 60,000,000 animals. Their range at this time covered some 3,000,000 square miles reaching from the Atlantic to the Pacific, and from the Great Slave Lake to the Gulf of Mexico.

Yet, with the settlement of America, this vast number of animals was reduced almost to zero in less than a century, principally by hunters. In 1900, there were but 800 bison alive in all America, of which 200 were captive animals within enclosures.

On the western plains, bison congregated in huge herds when climate and pasture compelled annual migrations. Ordinarily, however, the bands composing these vast assemblages were much scattered, moving about in single file, so that in early days the plains were criss-crossed by paths worn deeply into the soil; especially deep to and from watering places and over mountain passes.

On the western plains, bison congregated in huge herds.

The early explorers of the plains and mountains were thus able to follow "buffalo paths" nearly everywhere they wanted to go. The speed and agility of these heavy creatures, with big bulls weighing a ton, was astonishing. They also swam well, and crossed large rivers without hesitation.

Bison were remarkably harmless, considering their size and strength. Hunters on foot and horseback entered the herds with little precaution, and despite considerable pawing and snorting by the bulls, were seldom molested. This behavior, so different from that of most wild cattle, is explained by their gregarious instincts, leading them to bunch together against danger, and also by the lack of large predators on the American Plains.

Nothing to compare with the lions of the African plains was found in America, Hence, the American bison, and his passivity and herd instinct made him an easy prey for men with guns.

The woodland caribous, the American counterpart of the North European and Asiatic reindeer, occurred over much of the Great Lakes region in early days, although it was probably never numerous. A herd is still found in Ontario.

The last caribou was recorded on Isle Royale in Lake Superior around 1900. Caribou are midway in size between elk and white-tailed deer. Both sexes possess palmate antlers. They are wandering animals, keeping on the move in search of food, although the woodland caribou does not carry on the great migrations characteristic of the Old World reindeer and the American caribou of the Barren Grounds.

The last caribou was recorded on Isle Royale in Lake Superior around 1900.

Unlike other members of the deer family, the caribou is not confined to yards in winter, for its big, widely-spread feet enable it to travel over the snow instead of plowing through it. Woodland caribou were never important game animals in the region, even to the Indians before the coming of the white man.

Puma Once Found Here

Perhaps the most interesting of our vanished mammals in the Great Lakes region was the puma, also known as cougar, panther, painter, and mountain lion, and by other local appellations.

The puma is one of the handsomest of the cats, and also possessed the greatest north and south range of any land animal, once being found from Alaska to the tip of the South American continent in Patagonia.

Naturally, one would expect to find a great variety of size and color in a creature which ranged from the Atlantic to the Pacific and from Alaska to Patagonia. Yet this is not the case, and few species show such uniformity. Adult pumas have no spots or stripes, and the upper parts are of a uniform hue, which may vary from a pale foxy red to a slate blue. The color variation, as previously stated, has nothing to do with sex, age, season, or locality.

The throat, belly, and inside of the legs are white. As to size, apparently pumas never exceed eight feet from tip of nose to tip of tail, with the average about seven feet, and a weight of about 200 pounds.

Pumas are lithe, beautiful beasts, seldom seen by man except when pursued and treed by packs of trained dogs. Their natural prey seems to have been deer, but with the development of agriculture and stock raising the big cats learned to take cattle and horses. Such activities soon brought them into conflict with man's interests, and led to their destruction except in mountainous areas where hunting is costly and difficult.

Their natural prey seems to have been deer.

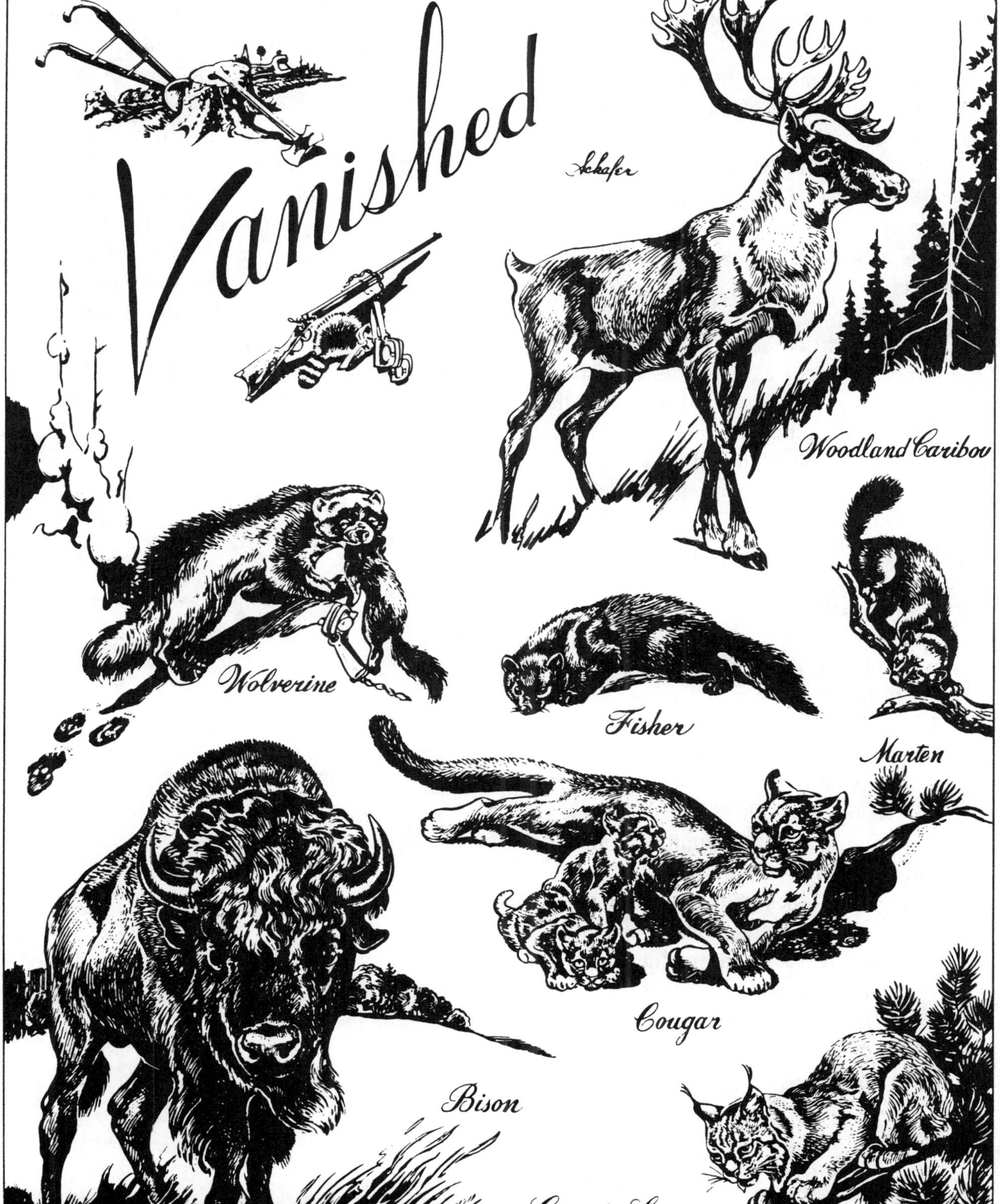
Vanished
Schafer
Woodland Caribou
Wolverine
Fisher
Marten
Cougar
Bison
Canada Lynx

Almost Incredible Feats

The strength and agility of the puma are legendary, and some of the feats attributed to them seem almost incredible. However, we must remember what our own domestic pussy cats can do, and then multiply that by twenty, since a puma is in all physical respects a cat, but twenty times as big and powerful.

This is not quite true of a lion or tiger, which are modified cats, but it is true of the puma. Like our cats, pumas are capable of an amazing burst of speed, but soon tire. Dogs are left behind as though standing still, but dogs will eventually tire out the puma and tree it. Like cats, pumas leap tremendous distances, 30-foot leaps having been frequently recorded on level ground.

One of the most curious features of the puma's life history is his attitude toward man. Here is a big, powerful courageous predator, able to attack man with success similar to the lion, tiger or leopard. Yet incidents of attack by pumas on humans are incredibly rare, either in North, South, or Central America.

The young are born in late winter or early spring, and usually number from one to four. The kittens are spotted, but the spots are lost as they grow up. They are weaned at three or four months, but may continue to travel with the mother until they learn to hunt for themselves, which may be when they are between one and two years of age.

Pumas have lived to be twenty years old in captivity and are believed to reach a similar age in the wilds unless killed by man or by accident.

The kittens are spotted, but the spots are lost as they grow up.

Probably the puma reached his greatest abundance in the hilly wooded country between the Mississippi River and the Allegheny Mountains, which teemed with deer and wild turkeys, and offered plenty of rocks and thickets for denning.

Another area of abundance was between the Coast Ranges and the Pacific from northern California to southern Alaska. At present, the puma is most abundant in the Sierras, Cascades, and Rocky Mountains where deer are still fairly numerous and where hunting is restricted by inaccessibility and the difficult terrain.

Animal Tracks

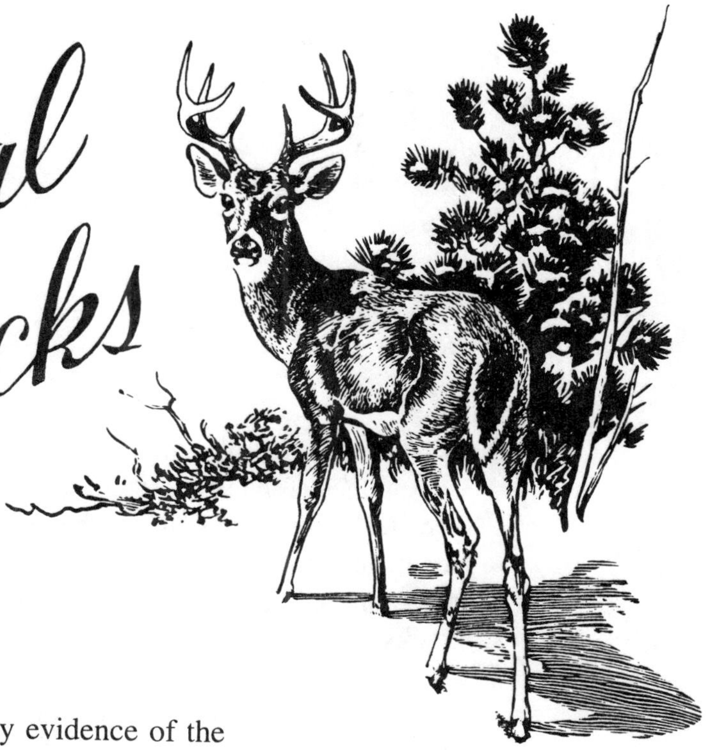

TRACKS are often the only evidence of the presence of wild animals. But tracks can provide information about their abundance, range, and habits.

The majority of wild animals are most active during twilight hours or at night, a principal reason why they are not seen more often.

To "know" an animal is to know the location of his home, his food, his enemies, and his habits. Tracks can help us understand these facets of animal ecology. Tracks are a record of activity and by close study, an observer can become intimately acquainted with an animal without ever having seen it.

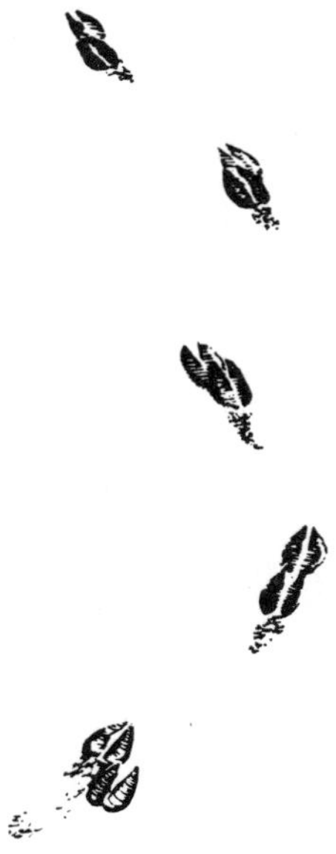

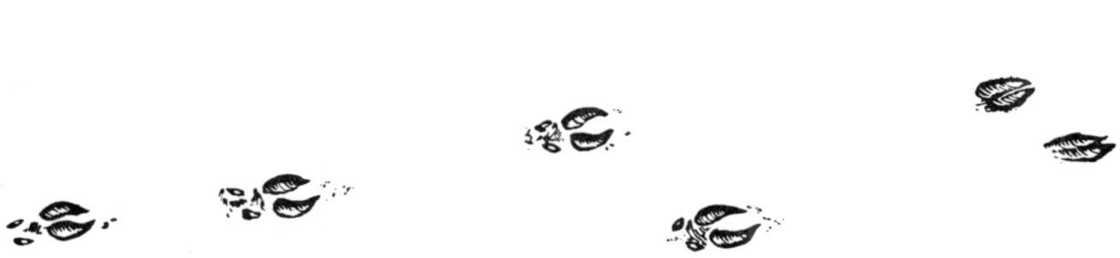

Schafer

Tracks of many animals are similar in appearance, for instance, the tracks of dogs, foxes, coyotes, and wolves. It is a help in the identification of such tracks to know which of these animals frequent the locality in which the tracks are found.

Tracks are best observed after rains, and in mud along streams banks, or following light falls of wet snow.

Tracks shown on the following pages are more perfect than are usually found under natural conditions. One can use them, however, to learn about the number, type, and nature of wildlife.

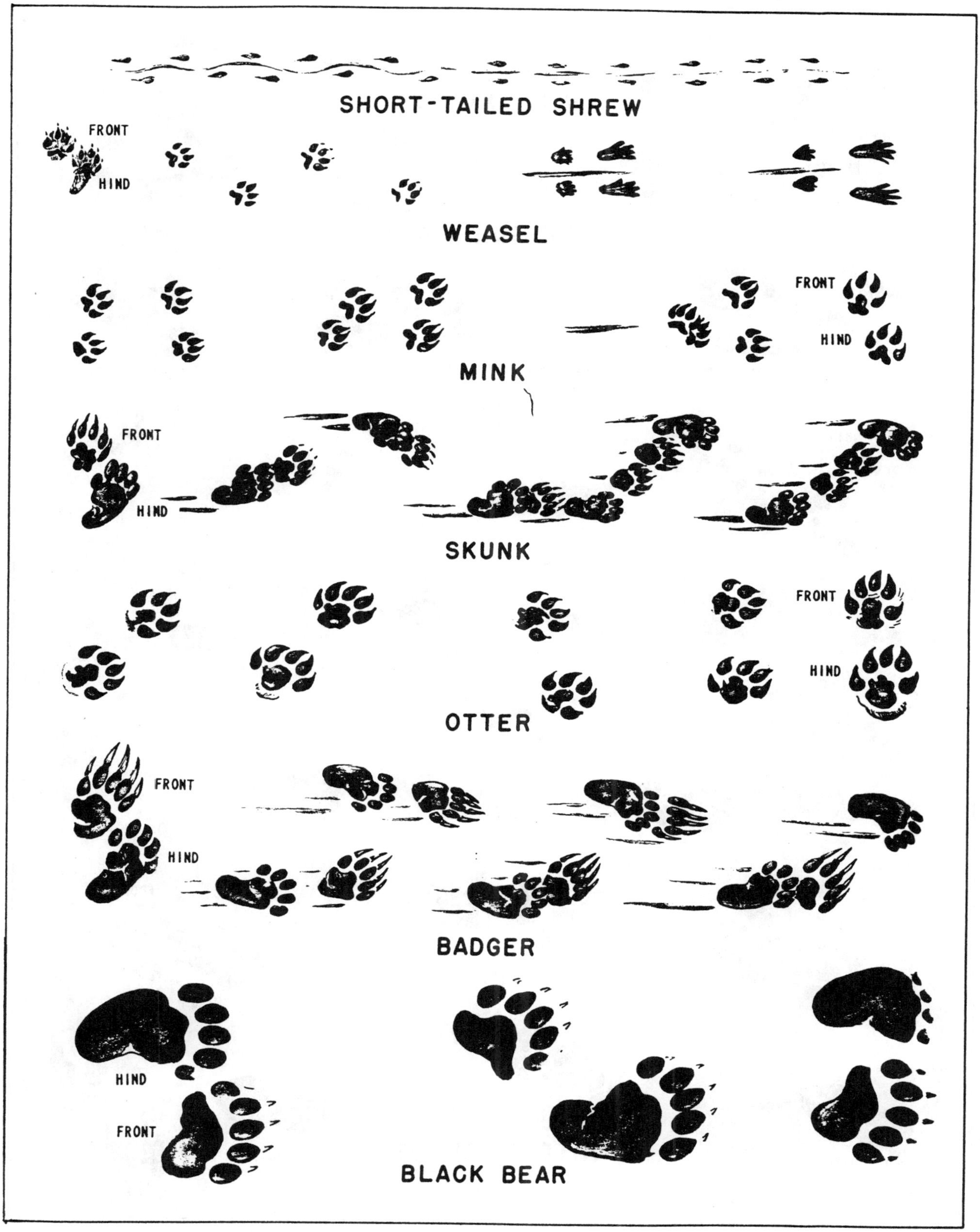
SHORT-TAILED SHREW
FRONT
HIND
WEASEL
FRONT
HIND
MINK
FRONT
HIND
SKUNK
FRONT
HIND
OTTER
FRONT
HIND
BADGER
HIND
FRONT
BLACK BEAR

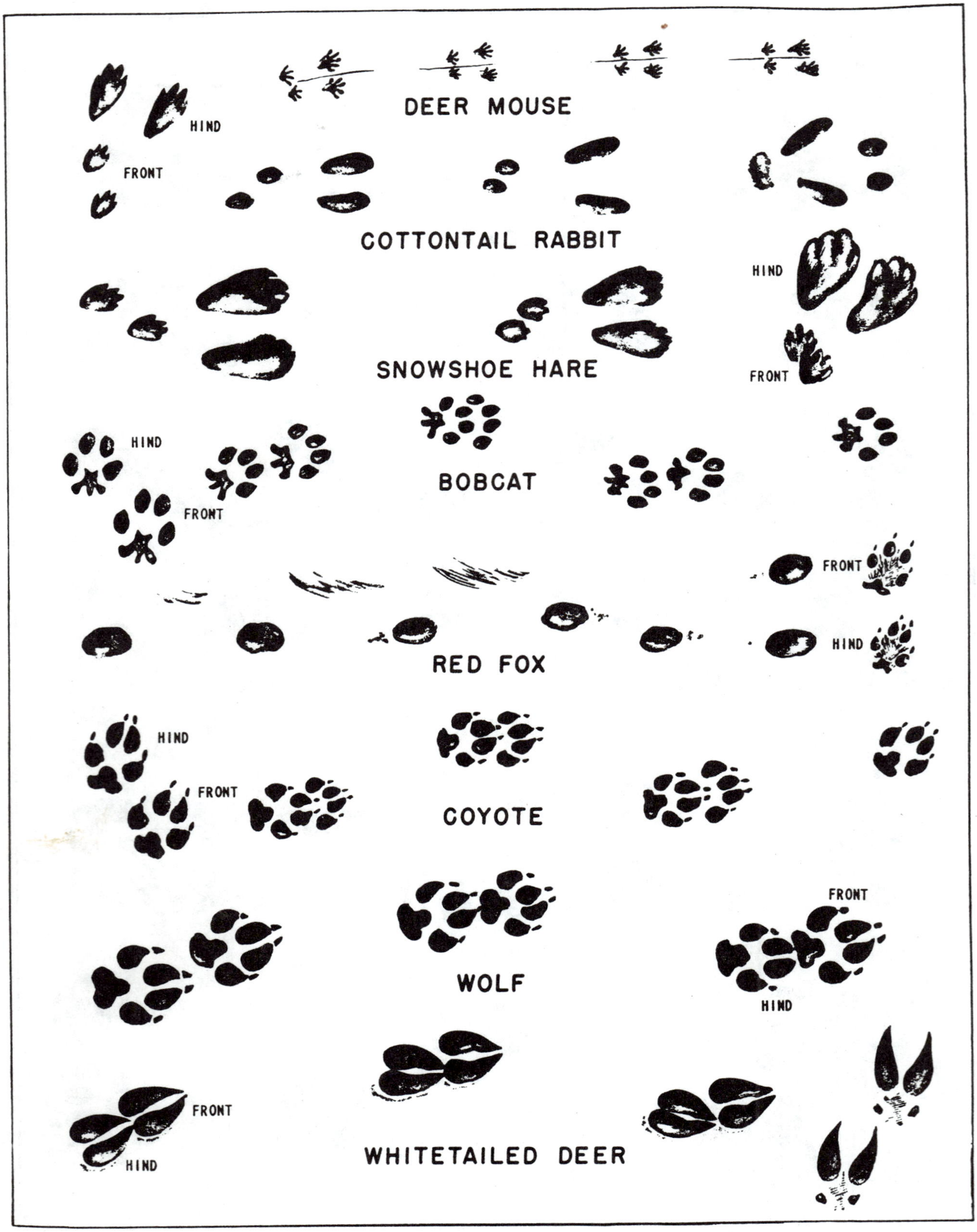
DEER MOUSE
HIND
FRONT
COTTONTAIL RABBIT
HIND
SNOWSHOE HARE
FRONT
HIND
BOBCAT
FRONT
FRONT
RED FOX
HIND
HIND
FRONT
COYOTE
FRONT
WOLF
HIND
FRONT
HIND
WHITETAILED DEER

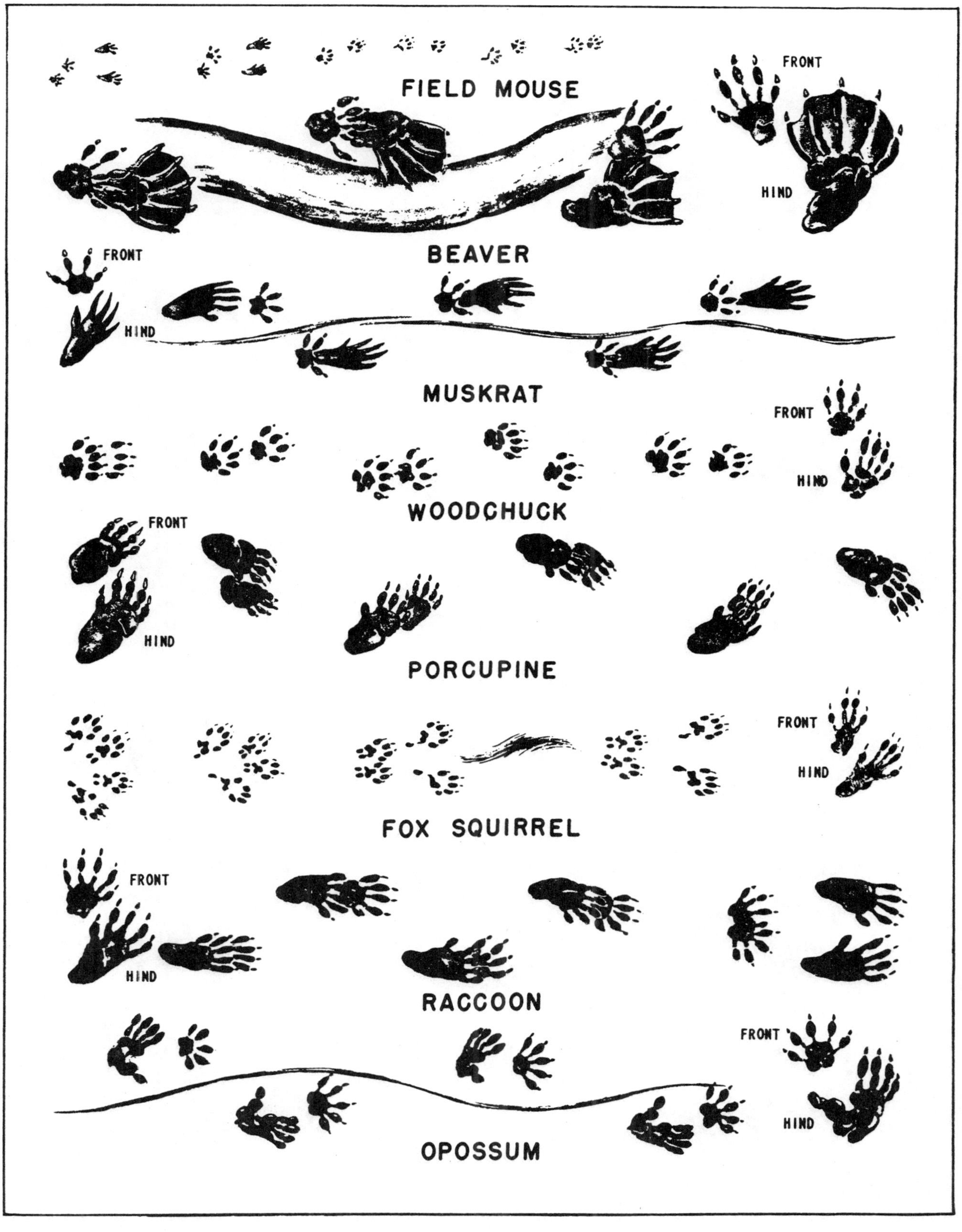
FIELD MOUSE
FRONT
HIND
BEAVER
FRONT
HIND
MUSKRAT
FRONT
HIND
WOODCHUCK
FRONT
HIND
PORCUPINE
FRONT
HIND
FOX SQUIRREL
FRONT
HIND
RACCOON
FRONT
HIND
OPOSSUM

Wildlife Ecology
A primer

Everyone enjoys watching deer graze in an open meadow or the antics of fox squirrels as they chase one another among tree branches. But the reality is that these animals--and all wild animals--are locked in a daily struggle for survival.

All wild animals have basic requirements--food, shelter, and water--and it takes much of their energy to locate and use these elements from their environment. For most animals, it is a full-time job to locate enough food, shelter, and water to survive and there is no time for games. Each species must find its own niche to secure these elements and it is within this niche that wild animals must work to survive.

Food

Each wild animal has its own food requirements, both in type and quantity. They also have developed special behaviors or physical adaptations to gather the food they require. For example, a squirrel has clawed feet and a bushy tail for balance that allow it to venture onto narrow branches for fruit and nuts. The squirrel has also learned to scavenge food on the ground and bury nuts for later consumption in cold weather.

Wild animals learn to seek out habitats that suit their food-gathering needs. Thus, you do not find fox squirrels in cedar swamps or badgers in deep forests. Some animals, notably white-tailed deer, require a mixture of habitats to suit their needs because deer are both grazers (in the summer) and browsers.

Some animals, to protect their species, establish feeding territories where animals of one species exclude other animals of that species in order to protect the available food in that area. It is a strategy designed to prevent overpopulation and protect the welfare of wildlife populations.

Sometimes, however, the notion of feeding territories can be detrimental to wildlife, such as in the case of moose, which require large areas of uncivilized territory to survive. Because man has reduced the habitat available to establish such large territories, some species are limited in population and may never again be very numerous in the region.

In many cases, the food in a particular area will vary from year to year. This may cause migration or even starvation, depending upon circumstances.

Sometimes, however, the notion of feeding territories can be detrimental to wildlife.

Shelter

Much is made of the woodchuck's ability to create holes that are suitable to shelter rabbits, fox, and other animals. It is indeed important for animals to have access to adequate shelter if they are to survive.

Adequate shelter protects animals from predators and harsh weather. Shelter is also required for reproduction, raising young, and sometimes feeding. And shelter can take many forms, depending upon the wild animal. Hollow trees, underground dens, brush piles, leaves, and thick grass all host wild animals.

Some animals, such as woodchucks and badgers, are able to make their own shelter if the soil is right. They are less dependent upon others for survival. But other animals, such as cottontail rabbits, are very much dependent upon the availability of brush piles, rock piles, and underground dens. Some squirrels, too, face a "housing shortage" in the treetops. Thus, one can see that there is a ready market for hollow trees and holes in the ground.

Some animals, such as woodchucks and badgers, are able to make their own shelter if the soil is right.

Water

In the Great Lakes region, water is generally plentiful. Water is available through the food wild animals eat or from the many lakes, ponds, rivers, and creeks that are found in the region.

Unlike the desert environment of the Southwest United States, water is generally not a limiting factor for wild animals in this region. As a result, one is unlikely to find many physical or behavioral adaptations among Great Lakes wildlife for water conservation.

Population Dynamics

It is the relationship between these three elements that determines the populations of wildlife species. In times when one or more of the elements of food, shelter, and water are scarce, wildlife populations decrease.

In the Great Lakes region, it can generally be stated that, because of the abundance of water in the region, that population ups and downs are primarily the result of a combination of food and shelter. Contrary to popular belief, it takes more than food alone to stimulate population growth.

It is normal for wildlife populations to undergo minor fluctuations from year to year and even within a year. For example, populations of wild animals are generally at their peak in late summer following the breeding season and before the stress of cold weather has set in. Also, deer, squirrel, and other animals that depend heavily on the production of acorns may see shifts in their populations during years of poor acorn production.

When all of the population fluctuations are averaged, then one can estimate the carrying capacity of a given habitat. The carrying capacity is the optimum number of a given species in a particular habitat.

Carrying capacity is strongly related to the basic elements required for wildlife survival. The

Carrying capacity is strongly related to the basic elements required for wildlife survival.

amount of food, shelter, and water in a particular habitat is crucial to determining how many animals may use that habitat. Sometimes, by altering these elements, the carrying capacity can be increased. For example, cottontail rabbits may increase in number if brush piles are constructed offering them additional shelter. If there is enough food to support more rabbits, then the population can be expected to increase.

Generally, because most wildlife populations are stable, there are about as many wild animals killed each year as are produced. This means that the life span of many animals in the wild is very short. But without mortality, we would soon be overrun with rabbits, mice, and raccoons.

Mortality

It is important to remember that life in the wild is a struggle for survival. There are several important mortality factors, in addition to exposure and starvation, that work against wild animals. These include predation, disease, and accidents.

Predation is rarely seen in the wild but occurs often. It occurs whenever one animal captures and consumes another and can give rise to a "chain" relationship between animals. For example, the star-nosed mole eats earthworms but it may be eaten by a badger, which in turn may be eaten by a wolf. This is called a food chain.

And predation can come from the skies, too. The hawks and owls of the Great Lakes region are effective predators and take their toll on white-footed mice to skunks and squirrels.

Wild animals have developed physical adaptations to help them avoid predation.

Wild animals have developed physical adaptations to help them avoid predation. One of the most effective of these is camouflage. The autumn, brown coat of the white-tailed deer, for example, makes it hard to spot against the forest backdrop. Perhaps the most famous of all camouflage is the changing color of the snowshoe hare, which sports a white coat in the dead of winter.

Some animals have behavioral adaptations that help them avoid predation. Many wild animals are nocturnal, that is, they are active only at night, which helps them avoid contact with humans, dogs, cats, and other potential enemies. The snowshoe hare and cottontail rabbit have learned to dodge pursuers so that it is more difficult to capture these wild animals.

Some animals have behavioral adaptations that help them avoid predation.

Still others, such as the porcupine and skunk, have developed offensive weapons that help them avoid predators.

Another mortality factor is disease. When populations of a species become very high, then disease tends to occur and reduce the population. This has been observed in snowshoe hares, coyotes, and raccoons.

Finally, many wild animals die accidentally. Squirrels fall from trees and deer are hit by cars. While accidents may take relatively few individuals, it is important to remember that just as in the human experience, wild animals must deal with bad luck.

Hunting

Despite all of the mortality factors, the population of wild animals in the fall is almost always greater than the carrying capacity. This means that many animals will not live through the winter and will die of either starvation or exposure. In the case of game animals, then, a decision must be made as to how to best manage this over population.

The white-tailed deer is an excellent example of how an animal can over populate an area and cause problems. Deer were introduced onto North Manitou Island in Lake Michigan in the 1920s and were the subject of annual deer hunts that attracted hunters to a resort. But the island was purchased by the U.S. Department of Interior to become part of the Sleeping Bear Dunes National Lakeshore.

During purchase negotiations and for a year afterward, no deer hunting was permitted on the island. The result: deer soon became so numerous in the fall that many starved to death in the winter. Also, the numbers of deer pressured them to eat virtually all vegetation they could reach. By the time of the first public hunt in 1984, the island vegetation was so damaged that it will take decades to recover.

In many cases, hunting is the most reasonable means of avoiding over population of game species. In autumn, hunting seasons are regulated to reflect the current condition of deer herds and other species. The result is that only the surplus animals are harvested, thus reducing the number of conflicts with man (car-deer accidents, for example) and winter starvation.

Human Conflicts

Wild animals have faced new challenges with the coming of the Europeans. First, there was extensive trapping to satisfy fashion, and then came settlement.

Today, more and more land is being consumed as urban sprawl continues to spread throughout the region. Already, the region has lost more than 50 percent of the wetlands it once had, and these wetlands were important breeding, nesting, and feeding habitats for many wildlife species.

As man continues to push wildlife to the edge, wild animals come in increasingly frequent contact with man. Bear, coyotes, and even wolves are showing up in people's backyards where they were once thought eradicated. In some cases these confrontations with man are little more than entertainment, but when large herds of deer destroy valuable crops, there is a cry for action.

In some cases, man's hunger for land has led to the complete eradication of some wildlife species. But just as man has caused extinction, so has he been able to reintroduce species. The elk, moose, pine marten, and fisher are examples of how man can use his knowledge to bring back animals once thought lost forever.

In the case of wolves, which were once thought extinct on the Michigan mainland, they have migrated from Minnesota and Wisconsin to repopulate most of the Upper Peninsula. Apparently, they have learned to adapt to man's presence.

There will continue to be challenges for our Great Lakes wildlife but with concerned and knowledgeable citizens, they will continue to flourish in the region.